# Turning Pupils on to Learning

CW00853818

*Turning Pupils on to Learning* documents and makes visible how creative learning approaches can engage and motivate children in their learning.

The book features six case studies of creative learning projects that cover the early years through to Key Stage 3, written by the teachers and creative practitioners involved. From the creation of new learning spaces to wider curriculum innovation, the case studies discuss the need for the projects, how they came about, the activities and challenges, and the lasting outcomes for teachers and pupils. They describe a model of learning that offers an ethical way for children to engage with the world, which develops their creative skills and supports high achievement.

Each case study is supported by a wealth of questions and activities designed to provoke personal reflection and professional development discussions with colleagues.

*Turning Pupils on to Learning* also features an accessible overview of the key issues and debates of the book. It comprehensively explains:

- what is meant by creativity, engagement and motivation in learning;
- the critical importance of developing a creative pedagogy;
- how to implement creative initiatives that motivate young people;
- the value of listening to young people's voices;
- how to influence school and classroom culture to engage pupils.

This practical book is an invaluable guide for all those involved in teaching and engaging young people.

**Rob Elkington** was Director of the Creative Partnerships, Birmingham programme and currently works for the Royal Shakespeare Company. He is a fellow of the Clore Leadership Programme and a Primary School Governor.

## Creative Teaching/Creative Schools Series

Series Editors: Pat Thomson, Julian Sefton-Green and Naranee Ruthra-Rajan

# Turning Pupils on to Learning

Creative classrooms in action

Edited by Rob Elkington

Routledge
Taylor & Francis Group

LONDON AND NEW YORK

First published 2012
by Routledge
2 Park Square, Milton Park, Abingdon, Oxon OX14 4RN

Simultaneously published in the USA and Canada
by Routledge
711 Third Avenue, New York, NY 10017

*Routledge is an imprint of the Taylor & Francis Group, an informa business*

© 2012 R. Elkington for selection and editorial material; individual chapters, the contributors.

The right of the editor to be identified as the author of the editorial material, and of the authors for their individual chapters, has been asserted in accordance with sections 77 and 78 of the Copyright, Designs and Patents Act 1988.

All rights reserved. No part of this book may be reprinted or reproduced or utilised in any form or by any electronic, mechanical, or other means, now known or hereafter invented, including photocopying and recording, or in any information storage or retrieval system, without permission in writing from the publishers.

*Trademark notice*: Product or corporate names may be trademarks or registered trademarks, and are used only for identification and explanation without intent to infringe.

*British Library Cataloguing in Publication Data*
A catalogue record for this book is available from the British Library

*Library of Congress Cataloging in Publication Data*
Elkington, Rob.
Turning pupils on to learning : creative classrooms in action / Rob Elkington. – 1st ed.
    p. cm.
  1. Creative thinking. 2. Creative activities and seat work.
  3. Classroom utilization. I. Title.
  LB1537.E55 2011
  371.3—dc22                                             2011011710
ISBN: 978-0-415-57773-1 (hbk)
ISBN: 978-0-415-57774-8 (pbk)
ISBN: 978-0-203-80346-2 (ebk)

Typeset in Galliard
by HWA Text and Data Management, London

MIX
Paper from
responsible sources
FSC® C004839
www.fsc.org

Printed and bound in Great Britain by the MPG Books Group

This book is dedicated to Nicky, Stevie and Tess.

# Contents

# Illustrations

## Figures

# Tables

# Contributors

**Jeremy Brown** has lived and worked in Wolverhampton for thirty years; his professional career began in theatre in education and drifted into film-making. He established Dialogue, a media company in 1988, and has produced programmes with schools, local authorities for the BBC and other broadcasters. More recently Jeremy has been involved with Creative Partnerships as a creative agent working in particular with Deansfield Community School where project-based learning has taken students and staff into nightclubs, on several trips abroad and, as illustrated in this publication, allowed for extensive work in regeneration and community cohesion.

**Angela Carlin** has worked at Lillian de Lissa Nursery and Belgravia Children's Centre for 18 years and has been the deputy head teacher for over four of these. Her work has taken her to Harvard University, Reggio Emilia, Bologna and Denmark to study many different pedagogies and teaching styles. She is a fully trained Forest School leader and supports all staff members in providing the most appropriate personalised learning opportunities for each child.

**Johanne Clifton** was head teacher at Allens Croft Primary School. She was appointed in 2006, having previously been a literacy coordinator with a passionate commitment to the use of literature in raising standards. On arriving at Allens Croft, she developed a clear ethos of creative learning and partnerships in order to develop an engaging and relevant curriculum through which children were excited by learning and so able to achieve high standards in writing. She has since moved to Billesley Primary school, also in Birmingham.

**Emma Davies** has been a primary school teacher, in various settings within Birmingham for the last nine years. Emma aims to give children a voice within her classroom and facilitates them to lead the direction of their own learning. Over the last three years she has worked closely with creative practitioners and facilitators on a wide variety of teaching and learning projects. Emma has been heavily involved in the writing of a child-led creative curriculum for Allens Croft.

**Rob Elkington** works for the Royal Shakespeare Company and is currently head of the RSC/Warwick University Centre for Teaching Shakespeare. Prior to this he worked as director of the Creative Partnerships, Birmingham programme, after working with the team to create and run a professional development programme in creative education for teachers and artists. He was one of the founders of the Play House, a drama and theatre company for young people and families in Birmingham, and ran it until 2002. He is a Fellow of the Clore Leadership Programme and Chair of Governors at Percy Shurmer Primary School.

**Jane Hanmer** was a nursery nurse for 24 years before studying and obtaining a first class honours degree in early years education and becoming a qualified teacher. She has taken part in a range of study tours including Reggio Emilia, China and Keffalonia where she has studied a range of pedagogical approaches. Jane is an aspiring Advanced Skills Teacher at Leighswood School in Aldridge where she leads a large Nursery team. Jane is a Forest School leader and has developed Forest School provision for all children in Nursery on the school site.

**Adrian Higgins** is a freelance creative practitioner and creative learning consultant to schools and colleges in the West Midlands. He has been working collaboratively with schools and colleges for 20 years. In partnership with schools he plans creative ways into curriculum content and support teachers in developing their practice. Adrian is passionate about promoting creativity as an effective learning strategy, and he also plans and delivers professional development that is connected to curriculum change and creative learning to both schools and the creative industries. These training programmes have been endorsed by Herefordshire School Improvement Services as well as the Creative Partnerships Programme.

**Rebekah Hooper** studied music at Royal Holloway College and worked as a freelance cellist prior to becoming a secondary music teacher and has taught at Lakers School for fifteen years. During this time she has held several posts including head of music, team leader for expressive arts and is now creative curriculum coordinator. In addition to this, over the last six years, she has worked for several organisations, including Creative Partnerships and has developed CPD programmes for teaching staff and arts practitioners and advised on approaches to student leadership and research. She has recently released her third CD with her band.

**Gill Hutchinson** has over 30 years' experience in community development work undertaken in urban, rural and coastal areas throughout England. She currently runs her own consultancy business mainly specialising in community engagement and capacity building for local authorities, government agencies and voluntary and community sector organisations. She uses the action research techniques that she has tried and tested in community settings to enhance the curriculum and allow young people to experience new ways of gathering data and information.

**Lorna Rose** took her master's degree at the Royal College of Art and is now a facilitator and researcher working in early years settings. She has been part of the Creative Partnerships teaching and learning programme for over six years. She is resident artist and vice-chair of governors at Lillian de Lissa Nursery and Belgravia Children's Centre. She has written on strength in diversity for E.Y.E magazine (May 2009) and a chapter for *The Routledge International Handbook of Creative Learning* (2011).

**Emily Smart** is a drama specialist currently working at Brannel School in mid Cornwall. For the last six years she has been following the aspirations of the school to use the performing arts to encourage confident and independent learners. Her approach to teaching has been greatly influenced by the school's creative partnership with the Royal Shakespeare Company and the power of the ensemble. She is currently completing a postgraduate diploma as part of a MEd in professional development at University College Marjon, Plymouth in the area of science and drama.

**Kat Vincent** has been teaching for five years and currently works at Brannel School in mid Cornwall. She has been working alongside the Royal Shakespeare Company as part of the Learning and Performance Network for the past three years, focusing on the impact of teaching Shakespeare using active methods. She has recently completed an MEd in professional development, encompassing a postgraduate diploma in teaching Shakespeare from the University of Warwick and a dissertation centred on the inclusion of students with special educational needs and disabilities.

# Series introduction

We live in creative times. As political aspiration, as economic driver, as a manifesto for school reform and curriculum change, the desire for creativity can be found across the developed world in policy pronouncements and academic research. But creativity in schools can mean many things: turning classrooms into more exciting experiences, curriculum into more thoughtful challenges, teachers into different kinds of instructors, assessment into more authentic processes and putting young people's voice at the heart of learning. In general, these aspirations are motivated by two key concerns – to make experience at school more exciting, relevant, challenging and dynamic; and ensuring that young people are able to contribute to the creative economy which will underpin growth in the twenty-first century.

Transforming these common aspirations into informed practice is not easy. Yet there are programmes, projects and initiatives which have consistently attempted to offer change and transformation. There are significant creativity programmes in many parts of the world, including France, Norway, Canada, South Korea, Australia and the United States of America. The English programme, Creative Partnerships (www.creative-partnerships.com) is the largest of these and this series of books draws on its experience and expertise.

This book, *Turning Pupils on to Learning: creative classrooms in action* is the third in a series of books, *Creative Teaching/Creative Schools*. The series is written for head teachers, curriculum coordinators and classroom practitioners who are interested in creative learning and teaching. Each book offers principles for changing classroom and school practice and stimulus material for CPD sessions. The emphasis is on practical, accessible studies from real schools, framed by jargon-free understandings of key issues and the principles found in more academic studies. Each volume contains six detailed 'case studies' written by practising teachers and other creative practitioners each describing a project they have introduced in their schools. These stories are complemented by accounts from learners themselves, making clear the benefit and value of these approaches to changing learning.

## What is creative learning?

When educators talk about creative learning they generally mean teaching which allows students to use their imaginations, have ideas, generate multiple possible solutions to problems, communicate in a variety of media and in general 'think outside the box'. They may also mean practices in which children and young people show that they have the capacities to assess and improve work, sustain effort on a project for a long period of time, exceed what they thought was possible and work well with others to combine ideas and approaches. Some may extend the notion to include projects and approaches which allow young people to apply their creativity through making choices about what and how they will learn, negotiating about curriculum and involvement in generating possibilities for and making decisions about school priorities and directions.

But while there may be commonalities about what creative learning looks like as and in students' behaviours, there may also be profound differences. The notion of creativity may be associated with particular subjects, such as those that go under the umbrella term of the arts, in which generating new, odd and interesting perspectives on familiar topics is valued and rewarded. Or it may be seen as integral to science where habits of transforming curiosity into hypotheses have a long history. Or it may be connected to business and the goal of schooling students to have strongly entrepreneurial dispositions and capacities. These interpretations – and many more – are all possible and legitimate understandings of creativity and creative learning.

Although the term 'creative learning' may be new and fashionable, it draws on older knowledge and values which have helped give it legitimacy and which frame its current meaning (see *The Routledge International Handbook of Creative Learning* and *Researching Creative Learning, Methods and Issues*).

We have expressed our understanding of Creative Learning as a series of 'manifesto' principles. They underpin all the volumes in this series.

Students' creative learning depends on a quality of education where

- all young people from every kind of background are equally recognised as being creative;
- learning engages young people in serious, meaningful, relevant, imaginative and challenging activities and tasks;
- young people are respected for their knowledge, experience and capabilities;
- young people have an individual and collective right to actively shape their education
- teachers have the power to support, adapt and evaluate learning experiences for students exercising their professional judgement;
- schools invest in teacher learning;
- schools build partnerships with creative individuals and organizations;
- schools enable young people to participate fully in social and cultural worlds;
- families and local communities can play an inspiring and purposeful role in young people's learning.

## Turning Pupils on to Learning: creative classrooms in action

This book's theme is engaging and motivating pupils to learn. It explores why schools have chosen to take up creative learning; how teachers and creative practitioners have worked together to introduce creative learning in their classroom or teaching site; what happened for pupils when they did and how staff are embedding these changes within their school culture. The six case studies are written by practising teachers and creative practitioners with a little help from the book editor, Rob Elkington.

## References

Sefton Green, J., Thomson, P., Bresler, L., and Jones, K. (eds) (2011) *The Routledge International Handbook of Creative Learning*, London: Taylor and Francis

Thomson, P., and Sefton Green, J. (eds) (2010) *Researching Creative Learning, Methods and Issues*, London: Taylor and Francis

# Who this book is for and how you might use it

This book is written for those who have an interest in promoting creativity in learning and developing partnerships with creative people who can work with them.

The book includes six case studies from schools, five of which have been designated *Schools of Creativity* as part of the Creative Partnerships programme.[1] To borrow a phrase from Dickinson *et al.* (2006) they are 'ordinary schools like yours and extraordinary schools like yours', striving to embed the systematic development of young people's creative abilities and skills in the education they offer to young people. The schools do not present themselves as experts but seek to share their knowledge with humility and generosity.

These schools are enquiring, ambitious and perhaps also courageous, prepared to innovate in order to improve the richness of school life and learning outcomes for their pupils and communities. The case studies have been written by the teachers, head teachers, creative practitioners,[2] artists, creative agents[3] and young people who have been directly involved in creative learning projects and they cover schools in early years, primary and secondary phases. It is their voices, experiences and reflections that are privileged in a belief in the power of peer to peer learning. They document with honesty what they did and why, who was involved, what resources were required, what happened in the partnerships and projects and reflect on what was achieved and the difference that they made. They do this in part out of a sense of duty to disseminate their findings but mainly from a wider interest to encourage colleagues to consider the case for creative learning in their own settings.

In my role as editor I have set out to frame the case studies in such a way that they enable you to see their relationship to the theme of the book, to evaluate the claims they make and to find the connections to your own setting and practice. You will see that I have inserted questions throughout the text to invite a moment of pause and thought if that is helpful, and then a series of open reflective questions at the foot of each case study that you can use to prompt discussion.

The case studies focus on activities designed to motivate and engage young people in their learning. They present different dimensions of what a creative classroom might feel and look like – and in doing so, they challenge the notion of what constitutes a classroom – and the implications for staff. This book offers rich 'thinking resources' to enable you:

- to reflect on your current practice;
- to ask questions to stimulate your critical thinking;
- to consider the different dimensions of engagement, motivation and creativity in learning.

The book is intended to support professional development. Each case study might be used for an hour long session and includes questions to prompt discussion and there are four ideas for more structured and extended sessions after Chapter 6. The book will be successful if it provokes debate and helps you to develop your own ideas about what you read and then inspires you to action.

## Notes

1 Creative Partnerships is a national creative learning programme established in 2002. It is designed to develop the skills of young people across England, raising their aspirations and achievements, and opening up more opportunities for their futures. It brings creative workers such as artists, architects and scientists into schools to work with teachers to inspire young people and help them learn (http://www.creative-partnerships.com/).
2 A practitioner from any cultural, commercial or industrial who demonstrates creative skills and works with schools to bring new creative and innovative approaches to teaching and learning. Source: *Reflections on a Creative Journey*, Cre8us, http://www.cre8us.org.uk/.
3 A practitioner drawn from the field above who works to support and challenge schools to plan, run and reflect on their Creative Partnerships activity.

# Acknowledgements

I would like to thank the contributors to this book for sharing their inspiring stories with such generosity and for their patience and persistence, and the series editors for their encouragement, challenge and guidance. I also want to acknowledge the influence on me of the ideas and wisdom of the many remarkable colleagues and collaborators I had the pleasure to work with in the Creative Partnerships programme and in particular Steve Ball, Maria Balshaw and Jonothan Neelands.

The photographs used in each chapter have been taken by the respective authors and are reproduced with their permission.

# Introduction

## Rob Elkington

This book privileges the voices and experiences of serving teachers and creative practitioners who are working every day to improve the life chances of the pupils in their school. In writing about their own practice the authors reflect on how to motivate and engage children in forms of learning that develops their ability to act and behave in creative ways. This is referred to throughout as *creative learning*.

The contributors to this book propose that creative learning is particularly effective at creating the conditions for learning that are meaningful to young people and which generate their motivation and long term engagement. The typical features of this are rigour, challenge, surprise, authenticity and the chance for children to shape what and how they learn in the pursuit of open ended outcomes.

Since the nineteenth century school systems across the world have become adept at taking millions of children from the ages of 4–18 through an education intended to send them into the world with the skills, knowledge and qualifications to participate in society. In England these desired outcomes are described in the Every Child Matters policy (2004) under five areas: children will stay safe, enjoy and achieve, be healthy, make a positive contribution and be economically independent and schools are inspected on the extent to which they secure these outcomes for children. As elsewhere, key components of the judgements made by school Inspectors are the standards of attainment that children achieve, as seen in test scores at the end of primary school and the number and grade of exam passes at age 16 with a benchmark of five A*–C passes, including Mathematics and English. The pressure exerted through the system to achieve continual improvement in these arguably narrow measures of a school's effectiveness is one familiar to many working in schools and has been influential in shaping school organisation, curriculum content, pedagogy and assessment.

For a number of the contributors working in primary and secondary schools this pressure had manifested in conformity and caution in their school which they believe resulted in many children feeling uninterested in learning that they felt held little relevance for them. Their common analysis is that to challenge this situation they had to be pro-active and take risks to introduce new practices that would engage children and motivate staff to change their way of doing things. For all of our authors this has been organised around the concept of developing children's creativity and introducing creative thinking across the curriculum.

If you have picked up this book it is likely that you are either a) curious to know something about creativity in the classroom and what that might mean for your practice or b) already some way down the track of introducing creative approaches in your teaching and are wanting new ideas (the 'magpie' tendency being one of features of creative people) or c) looking for resources to support wider change across your school. If any of these apply to you then I hope you will continue to read on, as this book has been designed with you in mind. It features six different case studies written by those working in schools – teachers, artists and other creative practitioners – from Early Years to Secondary level which gives an in depth example of practice. They are all stories of change and describe the development process as well as the outcomes of their work.

They were selected to reflect a range of different contextual challenges and different responses to a common issue. This essay sets out to introduce the key concepts of the book, the ideas of other writers and researchers, introduce the schools and the focus of each chapter and suggest ways that you might use this book with colleagues. Just to re-assure you, you don't have to read the whole thing in one sitting. In fact returning to different case studies after analysing and discussing the provocations of another will build your understanding of the field and should lead to better conversations and more informed action.

So let us turn first to think about the main concepts that underpin the book – creativity, motivation and engagement.

The current interest in creativity in schools is not new. It can be traced back through the twentieth century, for instance in arts education, in ideas about a play-based curriculum and in policy such as the Plowden Report (1967) into primary education under the notion of child-centred learning. What gave the current focus on creativity its impetus is an economic analysis embraced by the New Labour Government (1997–2010) that argued that future prosperity in the post-industrial future was in the production and exchange of symbolic goods such as software, music or design, the so called knowledge or 'weightless' economy. This kind of economy is dependent on human and intellectual capital, fast moving, unstable and hungry for novelty and innovation. For the UK to thrive in this world the economy would need workers with different kinds of skills and aptitudes than those traditionally nurtured in school. They would need the basics such as good literacy but also the skills to develop and apply ideas in different contexts, imagine and explore possibilities, question, be flexible, resilient and collaborative. These are the sorts of traits and behaviours that are required to be creative. The influential NACCCE report *All our Futures* (1999) found with some rare exceptions, that the education system was not geared up to promote this agenda and that it needed to be. It also argued that a more expansive cultural education, especially through the arts, was critical to the success of young people to thrive in an increasingly complex and dynamic world.

Another driver behind the creativity agenda is the concern that too many children are failed by schools, where they experience uninspiring teaching within a narrow curriculum which bears little relevance to their lives. For those setting education policy the focus on developing pupil creativity was another way of achieving more effective classrooms where pupils make good progress and their standards of attainment improve. OfSTED reports have found evidence to support this view.[1]

So what is creativity? Creativity is concerned with action and the idea that action is formative; by acting in and upon the world you fashion it and change it.

The definition proposed by NACCCE (1999) and now widely used in the education system is 'imaginative activity fashioned so as to produce outcomes that are original and of value'. Creativity involves using the imagination to produce new ideas and applying those ideas to produce an outcome within a particular domain of human activity – for instance fiction writing, politics, advertising or cooking – that proves to be new and valuable. Whether the level of novelty has to be historically original i.e. new to the world or just new to the person involved, depends on what you believe creativity is and whether you think, for instance, it is the preserve of the genius or you hold a more democratic notion that it is a quality available to everyone.[2]

It will save a good deal of confusion if you consider that there is no universal, fixed or shared meaning of creativity. It is a concept constructed in specific and particular cultural contexts so will mean different things in different contexts, which Neelands and Choe (2010) suggest, can ultimately lead to the point that it can mean whatever you want it to mean. Banaji et al (2006) identify different rhetorical positions on creativity which amplifies this point; they are in tension with each other and vie to be accepted as the 'right' one.

The issue of what is understood by creativity is rarely considered so I suggest that it becomes a starting point for discussion and ongoing conversation to establish a shared set of understandings and principles. What do you understand (or choose) creativity to mean? How does it relate to your own context and school values and to the kinds of outcomes that you aspire to for your young people?

This volume represents a diversity of approaches and understandings of creativity – from the distinctive play, exploration and discovery practice of the early years practitioners at Lillian de Lissa, through an arts-led understanding at Allens Croft Primary School to Deansfield Community School where creativity stands for creative thinking applied in the real world.

Creativity is a quintessentially human quality and is associated, at least in education policy, as wholly progressive and positive. However human creativity can also be applied to achieve negative, anti-social and destructive ends if it is not developed within an environment of pro-social, positive values. In short, exploring the values of how and where creativity can be applied in the world is as important as learning about what it is and how it is encouraged and developed.

The position on creativity the authors have chosen is a reflection of their ethics and values (whether consciously so or not) and therefore influential in the design, staffing and purpose of their work. For instance the case study from Brannel School (Chapter 2) recounts how two teachers developed a creative pedagogy for the teaching of Shakespeare. Part of this story is about their teaching becoming more effective (as seen in pupils' attainment in their exams) but the other part is about their struggle to develop an *ensemble* classroom based on the values of mutual collaboration, respect and trust which model a way of being in the world.

## How do teachers learn to do creative learning?

The learning theories of John Dewey and Lev Vygostky both support creative approaches. Dewey not only argued that active, varied and social experiences were integral to anchor learning, but also that the child's experiences needed to be explicitly connected to the school curriculum and not left separate from it. Vygotsky focused on the kinds of social learning experiences that maximised learning; he is particularly known for his notion of the zone of proximal development – the area between what a child already knows and can do and what they can achieve – and the importance of appropriate and timely scaffolding – the provision of supports to help the child construct new knowledge. If these learning theories underpin a creative pedagogy what practical steps and conditions are required for teachers to develop creative learning in their schools? In the case studies the authors identify the following factors as being significant:

## Transforming the idea of a classroom

Teachers consistently draw on the disciplines of the creative partners they work with, not necessarily 'stealing' ideas but letting their classrooms (or for many outdoor sites for learning) be shaped by the ethos and practices of a different domain. So we see a classroom become like a theatre rehearsal room or an artist's studio where creative behaviours are required, and the value of what is produced is assessed in ways appropriate to the domain.

## Broadening experiences and knowledge

Many of our authors were able to travel in order to be inspired and provoked by practice in settings different from their own. For some it was a revelation to meet colleagues in the same neighbourhood while others went further afield to the source of specific types of practice, such as the pre-schools of Reggio Emilia or to the Forest Schools in Denmark (see Chapters 4 and 5). This was always undertaken as a collegiate activity, to allow reflection with colleagues on experiences and how they might be used to inform new practice. This is representative of our authors' 'commitment to engaging in high quality Continuing Professional Development (CPD) and in some cases, to postgraduate study.

## Support for teachers to lead change

Certain conditions were created to enable teachers to meaningfully lead change. All the projects and initiatives were given the resources required to grow and funding was matched with protected time for planning and reflection. In the case of Lakers School (Chapter 6) Rebekah Hooper was given one and a half days off timetable each week to lead a project aspiring to whole school change. The capacity of the staff team she worked with grew as they learnt new pedagogical approaches, new skills in coaching, leadership and developing their own and their pupils' emotional intelligence. The support of senior leaders was critical to this sustained and open ended endeavour.

## Understanding the costs of change

Our case studies show that a creative pedagogy requires teachers to take risks and to be resilient in the face of setbacks as they introduce new and unfamiliar practice and invite pupils to take a greater role in their learning. However there is another kind of risk that Kat Vincent (Chapter 2) reminds us of, the risk that creative learning may negatively impact on the attainment of pupils as measured in exams and tests. This can have serious personal and career consequences for a teacher. Clarifying the aim of creative learning approaches and deciding how success will be measured are therefore key issues to be agreed in order to support the teacher taking a risk.

## How do we understand engagement

The specific challenge for the contributors was how to motivate and engage children in their learning. They knew that there was more that pupils could and should achieve and doing more of what they were currently doing wasn't the answer. We can all remember and probably describe with some vehemence the experience of being bored in school and switched off from both what and how we were being taught. Visualise a moment when you have seen a class of young people powerfully motivated and totally engaged in their learning. Where are they? What are they doing? What do you notice about the quality of interaction and attention? What about the energy levels and the way children look? How high are the noise levels? What words would you use to describe what you see, hear and feel? Each of our case studies gives an insight into how the authors have moved towards the ideal you have been imagining (or re-living) and taken risks to create the kinds of necessary conditions which include environment, curriculum, pedagogy and partnerships.

So why are pupils bored? In an analysis of 15,000 entries to a *Guardian* newspaper competition in 2001 called *The School I'd Like* children and young people were in no doubt. It is due to a curriculum that is formulaic, teaching that is dull, relationships that are poor, lessons where children make no progress and don't understand how to do so, and a school where their needs are not recognised. The opposite of boredom is engagement and this is generated by an intrinsic fascination in a task that connects to one's interests, needs and aspirations. While this can and should be enjoyable, there is a difference between teaching that aims to make lessons more fun and that which aims for pupil engagement with learning. Fun may be generated by the way that a teacher behaves, by the kinds of pupil behaviour that is encouraged or by the playfulness of a task. It can be short term, short lived and be concerned with teaching the same (maybe dull) content in a more 'fun' way. Engagement requires pupils to make a deeper and personal connection to learning, the sort of connection that leads them to be fully absorbed in a task, turn up early for lessons, stay late afterwards and continue their work in their own time. Creative learning may be fun, but its most important contribution is to engagement. Engagement is absolutely necessary for deep and sustained learning; fun is not. Engagement occurs when tasks are meaningful and challenging.

Mihaly Csíkszentmihályi (1997) describes the ideal (but rare) experience of full engagement as being in a 'flow' state, and describes the conditions that bring this about:

> Flow tends to occur when a person's skills are fully involved in overcoming a challenge that is just about manageable. Optimal experiences usually involve a fine balance between one's ability to act and the available opportunities for action. If challenges are too high one gets frustrated, then worried and eventually anxious. If challenges are too low relative to one's skills one gets relaxed, then bored. If both challenges and skills are perceived to be too low, one gets to feel apathetic. But when high challenges are matched with high skills, then the deep involvement that sets flow apart from ordinary life is likely occur.
>
> (Csíkszentmihályi, 1997, p. 30)

As you read through the case studies you might want to think about the extent to which pupils achieve this balance of challenge and skills in your setting and the role of adults in giving guidance and support.

Another way to think about engagement is tapping into the concealed and discretionary effort of young people, the commitment and energy which they choose to bring to school or not. Many children are able to play the school game and even though they may be bored at times by their work they know that once it is completed, it will serve their aspirations to progress into higher education and employment. These children arrive in school with a healthy stock of social and cultural capital which can be characterised here as having access to networks and connections and possessing the attitudes and knowledge required to thrive in the education system. These advantages are transmitted (often unconsciously) to children through their parents and support their social mobility and ability to achieve within society. This can lead to children having a sense of high self-efficacy (discussed in more detail below) who are skilled at conforming sufficiently to the behavioural norms of schools to get from it what they want. However many children are not in this position, as described by the case study from Allens Croft Primary

School. It follows that continually seeking new ways to motivate and engage such children is a duty for schools in tackling inequality and closing the achievement gap between rich and poor. This is of critical importance to schools that find themselves in challenging circumstances or work with communities experiencing disadvantage.

We turn now to consider another aspect of our theme, the pre-requisite for engagement, and that is motivation.

## How do we understand motivation?

Motivation can be thought of as the stimulus or impulse to take action, while engagement is the process of staying the course of becoming fascinated by and locked into an activity. We can all recognise what it feels like to be motivated (and de-motivated) to do something and there are as many triggers as there are people. It could be born from challenging an injustice, proving someone wrong, a deadline, striving to improve or doing something that is enjoyable and that you are good at. Think about what keeps you motivated both personally and as a practitioner.

It's unlikely to be working on your own all day, to a centrally prescribed curriculum, a standard lesson shape, to children in rows of desks, where every child is assumed to learn in the same way at the same pace in chunks of 40 minutes just so they can pass exams. Although that's an extreme picture I'm sure you get the idea and this moves us into the territory of deep motivation and moral purpose. How often do you get the chance to work in ways that tap into your deeper motivation to be an educator? What would need to change for you to be able to work like that more of the time?

Monique Boekarts (2010) helps us to think about the way that motivation is shaped and triggered. She argues the role that motivation and the emotions play in the learning of students has been greatly overlooked but they are critical to learning new knowledge and skills in a meaningful way.

She suggests that the building blocks of motivation lie with our 'motivational beliefs'. These are views that we hold about ourselves – often unconsciously – and are formed through our sense of self and shaped by our positive and negative experiences in different areas of activity, or domains, like chemistry or dance for instance. A motivational belief is a view we hold about ourselves within that domain (e.g. 'I've got two left feet') and also about the effect on us of the different ways in which we are taught. The different elements that work together to construct a motivational belief are set out in Table 0.1.

Boekarts stresses that 'motivational beliefs are important because they determine the choices students make as well as how much effort they will invest and how long they will persist in the face of difficulties.' These beliefs are shaped by our direct experiences and by what is said to us by our teachers, friends, peers and parents. It is slightly depressing news that these beliefs tend to decline as we grow up as we observe and compare ourselves to our peers.

The good news is that teachers can positively impact on the motivational beliefs of students by setting expectations that are just higher than their current level of performance, communicating this clearly and providing the kinds of guidance that

**Table 0.1** Boekarts' elements of motivational beliefs

| | |
|---|---|
| Self-efficacy | Beliefs we have about our innate ability and competence |
| Outcome expectation | Beliefs that some courses of action will work and others will fail |
| Goal orientation | Beliefs about whether we see an activity as having a purpose |
| Value judgements | Beliefs about whether we are interested or not |
| Attribution | Beliefs about the causes of why we do well or don't succeed |

Source: Boekarts, 2010, p. 94

encourage self-reflection on the strategies and skills required to solve problems. The bad news is that it can be corrosive to a pupil's motivation if they attribute failure to their own lack of ability rather than choosing the wrong strategy, which conversely, can be motivating. Boekarts concludes that pupils are motivated to engage in learning when they:

- feel competent to do what is expected;
- perceive stable links between actions and achievement;
- value the subject and have a clear sense of purpose;
- experience positive emotions towards learning activities.

(Boekarts, 2010, p. 93)

## Funds of knowledge

There are positive actions that teachers can take to motivate pupils by understanding and valuing the knowledge they bring into school from their home lives, a rich but often ignored resource of culturally developed knowledge and skills. This knowledge can then be used by teachers to connect with pupils in culturally meaningful ways by reflecting on it in their curriculum and into creative learning activities. This concept is defined as drawing on children's 'funds of knowledge' (González *et al.*, 2005) and assumes that each teacher needs to know something distinctive and special about each child in their class. This may mean that teachers become researchers and pro-actively meet their pupils' families in their homes and communities rather than meeting on school premises in the teacher's environment. It might mean that teachers find ways to understand and value student' home and community knowledges through activities such as story-making and through active homework, where what family members know is integrated with school knowledge. Schools can also invite families to be part of the school and to contribute what they know about history, geography, science and so on.[3]

## Meaning and motivation

The issue of value and how to motivate change across an entire education system is the core concern of Michael Fullan's (2007) influential review of the research findings on school change. His central message is unequivocal – in order to motivate people, opportunities have to be created in order for them to make meaning of what they are doing. This is especially critical for new or change initiatives and the case studies in this book fall into that category. There are two elements to this. Making meaning is an ongoing process during an activity and so it is critical that opportunities for *formative* discussion and reflection are provided while 'doing'. It is also an outcome of an activity and therefore opportunities for participants to engage in *summative* reflection are also required. Learning therefore occurs through action and having the space to reflect on the new activity we have been engaged in. All our insights stem from reflective action.

The following observation by Fullan has an audience of teachers in mind but it applies equally to young people who are involved as co-constructors of learning in creative learning projects:

> Finding moral and intellectual meaning is not just to make teachers feel better. It is fundamentally related to whether teachers are likely to find the considerable energy required to transform the status quo. Meaning fuels motivation; and know how feeds on itself to produce ongoing problem solving.
>
> (Fullan, 2007, p. 39)

So the point here is that the task in hand has to hold relevance and be important in some way. I am sure you recognise the way that making progress and becoming better at something feeds the personal significance of what you are doing, and this is reinforced by having this success recognised. It makes you feel better and increases your self-confidence. To be able to make progress requires the development of the necessary skills, access to relevant resources and the development of knowledge about the task so that learning is incremental and happens within a clear context. This rigour applies equally to creative learning, which is concerned with applying the imagination, not letting it endlessly wander and wonder.

## Dignity, respect and emotions

Another key to generating motivation is paying careful attention to people's feelings through showing respect and building trust. This goes to the heart of the ethos of classrooms and the way it is expressed in the behaviours of adults and young people. The research by Ruddock *et al.*, (1996) suggests that students who are not respected are less motivated to learn and so schools that build trust between teachers and pupils are more likely to motivate them. The kinds of behaviours that promote respect and trust are socially based and Kanter (2004) suggests they involve making connections in new ways through conversation, carrying out meaningful work collaboratively, communicating respect and demonstrating inclusion.

Fullan (2007) proposes that the solution to motivating people is to create the conditions in which there is a careful balance of what he calls *tightness* and *looseness*. *Tightness* involves creating focus for an activity such as defining parameters, giving a clear direction for action and applying sufficient pressure to make progress. This is combined with enough *looseness* so that the right physical and intellectual resources are provided at the right time, which is not necessarily the pre-planned time. This needs to be afforded within an ethos of respect and trust so that progress can be made.

If you have any lasting doubts that these things matter then it is the voices of young people that offer the most powerful arguments. In 1967 *The Observer* ran a competition asking for young people's views on the school of their dreams and their hopes for the future. This was repeated in 2001 by Catherine Burke and *The Guardian* newspaper resulting in a publication called *The School I'd Like* (2003) comparing and reflecting on the two sets of responses. This book serves as an urgent call to action about the costs of neglecting children's voices from school development and finds that, despite constant reform to policy and teaching practice, the school experience of children and teachers has changed very little. Children are clear on what they want from school and call for a curriculum driven by 'adventure, curiosity and collective endeavour' across a wide range of human affairs. This impulse to explore and to be creative is a powerful motivation for young people as Oliver, 13, from Loughborough expresses with great eloquence:

> Students learn concepts by doing – smelling, seeing, hearing, touching and tasting as well as thinking either creatively or logically. All their senses are utilized in all sorts of manners so that learning is meaningful and practical – not something so alien that they have to be forced upon to do. When children find learning meaningful, they will naturally want to learn more and hence, they will be self-motivated and do not need to be pushed by adults to learn.
>
> (Burke and Grosvenor, 2003, p. 68)

This call for respect runs through 'The Children's Manifesto' crafted by Dea Birkett to summarise the themes of the 15,000 entries to the 2001 competition:

## The school we'd like is

- A beautiful school
- A comfortable school
- A safe school
- A listening school
- A flexible school
- A relevant school
- A respectful school
- A school without walls
- A school for everybody

I hope this selective look at the literature around our major themes has given you a clear framework to consider the evidence of the case studies and aroused your interest sufficiently to read them. Let us now turn to the ideas at heart of this book and give you a brief overview of the case studies.

## Chapter 1: Allen's Croft Primary School

Allens Croft staff share their approach to evidencing the impact on standards of a project with Year 3 pupils inspired by Philip Pullman's *Northern Lights* trilogy designed to challenge pupil passivity and promote their creativity. It shows how pupil tracking data and ongoing assessment provided the school with the evidence to argue for the value of the work. Their central insight is that connecting pupils to things they care about will generate engagement and that the outcomes can and should be evidenced.

## Chapter 2: Brannel School

This chapter focuses on how an English teacher and a Drama teacher developed a new creative pedagogy in order to motivate and improve students' learning in the complex texts of Shakespeare. It illustrates what sustained pupil engagement might look like and shares strategies for building motivation through the pursuit of a meaningful outcome. The authors highlight the links between the social health of the classroom and the level of children's ownership of an ambitious collective endeavour.

## Chapter 3: Lillian de Lissa Nursery School

This chapter focuses on how the all female nursery staff changed their thinking and practice to stimulate boys' curiosity and their creative and language development. Introducing more male practitioners into the setting, such as engineers and storytellers was a crucial change. The chapter argues that the ongoing practice of staff observing and documenting the boys' interests was critical to them learning about the kinds of provocations and resources that would engage them and extend their learning.

## Chapter 4: Deansfield Community College

This chapter is a case of how the school regards and exploits the potential of its neighbourhood and locality as a source and site for creative learning through 'real world' partnerships with business and voluntary organisations. It documents a controversial consultation project with a local Housing Association and argues that pupil motivation to learn is enhanced by the level of accountability of the work that young people produce and their public recognition.

## Chapter 5: Leighswood Primary School

This case study shares why and how an Early Years department set out to transform their outdoor space and re-imagine its potential for the creative development of children. In their view such physical developments have to be tied into rigorous pedagogical and curriculum thinking and that there is no greater resource for this than the interests and ideas of the children themselves.

## Chapter 6: Lakers School

This is a case of how a 'stuck' school set about engaging and motivating passive students in learning and in school life. It charts the process of re-building staff morale and changing the curriculum and timetable. The account sets out some required factors to make such a change: the necessity of engaging the energy and ideas of the community; caring for people's emotions; building relationships and committing to a long term process.

The combined core message of these chapters strongly relates to the research discussed here and forms the basis of a manifesto for creative learning: creative pedagogy is at the heart of engagement; find the evidence to argue it works; re-define the classroom in a 'real world' context; strive to include the excluded; change is less risky than staying the same and engage children by listening to them.

What might you write in your manifesto?

# 1

# Of dreams and curiosity
## What works and how do we know?

Johanne Clifton, Emma Davies and

Adrian Higgins, Allen's Croft Primary School

## Editor's introduction

This case study documents how Allens Croft Primary School in Birmingham set about using an immersive creative learning project as a means to engage Year 3 children as leaders of their own learning after a schooling experience that had encouraged passivity. In order to build the credibility of the innovation the leadership recognised the necessity of building confidence in new ways of working to both internal and external stakeholders. Their response to this was to use tracking data to evidence impact on attainment in writing to support their own observations on well-being and the attitudes of the children. However they were surprised by the extent and power of pupil ownership in the project. The elements of their challenge can be characterised as:

- the pressure to increase attainment in writing across the school;
- the need to counter the passivity of Year 3 children in lessons;
- an inquiry to develop a model and teaching approach that might do that;
- finding the right mix of assessment to show impact.

## Who's who?

- *Adrian Higgins* creative practitioner/visual artist
- *Andrew Tims* creative agent
- *Emma Davies* teacher

- *Johanne Clifton*   head teacher
- *Birmingham Rep Theatre* the education and backstage team in a production of Philip Pullman's *Northern Lights*

## The school context and key issues

## Johanne Clifton

- *Name* Allens Croft Primary School
- *Location* Brandwood, Birmingham
- *Age range* 5–11
- *No. on roll* 250
- *Website* www.allcroft.bham.sch.uk

Allens Croft Primary is a school committed to the process of developing creative learning to drive forward our school improvement. It has been on a journey of profound change – from issues with low standards and motivation to a school that is buzzing with ideas and children that are achieving national averages (and better) despite low attainment on entry. This has been due to a commitment by the whole school to creating an exciting and engaging curriculum which is tracked closely against children's progress in core skills. However school improvement is a never ending battle against national targets and the risk is that the learning experience of the children can become one driven entirely by numerical targets.

Allens Croft is in a challenging context, being in the highest quintile for social and economic deprivation and poverty indicators in England, with 92 per cent of our families in the highest group for childhood poverty indicators.

## Raising aspirations and firing the imagination

As head teacher my own beliefs are very much centred on raising aspirations and setting high expectations. I am a passionate believer in the power of stories and spend much of my own time reading, sharing and telling stories – fantasy stories, fairy tales, family stories and histories.

Stories are important in so many different ways. By listening to a story you enter into a world where anything is possible; you are taken in by the narrative, however impossible and escape from the here and now. For our children this is essential, not just in improving their own ability to write but in what they dare to dream. We all construct our own stories – our life stories, our beliefs about ourselves and our hopes for the future. These are intrinsically tied up with self-esteem and self-perception and it is vital for our children to dream outside the limitations and perspectives of the Allens Croft estate. On one level, to inhabit the world of the imagination and on another, to dream of what is possible in oneself. These ideas are the foundation of the project described below which emerged through a careful analysis of what we needed to do to continue to improve our school and it marked a turning point in the development of our philosophy and practice as a school.

## How do we improve writing?

In 2008, despite the use of a range of literacy and numeracy intervention programmes, results at the school had not risen enough and there were considerable issues of motivation and engagement in learning, as well as in developing partnerships with our families and the community.

We knew from our data and from our children's enjoyment in school that we were making a difference to core standards but we still found writing the most challenging area to improve. Yet to make a sustained difference we had to find out what the real issues were and our analysis found that the quality of children's basic language structures and vocabulary needed to be improved. One response was to extend the school day to allow more time for sharing stories but more was needed, and this was engaging children in their work. Therefore we chose to focus on our Year 3 class to develop new creative learning practice which might innovate on behalf of the whole school.

## Purposeful innovation

The Year 3 class identified for the project were a class of two contrasting halves and both vulnerable. One half (11 children) had been identified in Reception as 'more able' from their Foundation Stage results but by the end of Year 2 only five of them were achieving above national averages. The other half of the class was low achieving or children with special needs.

The quality of teaching they had received in their early years was not of a high quality and in order to 'catch up', teaching had become highly structured and focused. The outcome of this was that the class had become profoundly passive, always waiting for the teacher to tell them what to do and how to do it, or simply not doing it at all. They could read and write well but wouldn't stretch themselves or offer their own ideas. We hadn't stimulated their imaginative capacities or enabled them to apply those they had shown to their learning. We needed to look closely at how to motivate the class and at our curriculum offer. These were children that we were failing.

## Targeting and building the evidence base

Pupil targets are set in the traditional way, against attainment on entry and expected outcomes at the end of the year and Key Stage but we aim for accelerated progress against national averages. Each term the head and deputy spend half a day with each class teacher analysing the well-being, progress and learning of the class and identifying how provision can be better personalised to meet the needs of children. In the case of our Year 3 class we proposed an extended project with a creative practitioner.

In order to develop a shared understanding of the impact of creative learning on standards and motivation we have developed a specific way of tracking pupil progress throughout the school and we wanted to test this further in this project.

Do you recognise this analysis of pupil needs? To what extent is engaging in a creative learning project about promoting values as well as an instrumental response to an educational issue?

## Timeline

- *December 2008* Initial planning meeting involving Andrew, Johanna and Emma. Contracting of Adrian and Birmingham Rep.
- *February 2009* Detailed planning discussions and involvement of Birmingham Rep and Adrian.
- *March 2009* Visits to Birmingham Rep for backstage tour and to see both parts of *His Dark Materials*.
- *February–April 2009* Six weekly whole day sessions, regular planning and reflection sessions between Adrian and Emma.

## Engaging a creative practitioner

I had met Adrian Higgins and discovered that he was using learning journals to involve children in reflecting on their own learning. He used journals in a formal way to collect and comment on ideas to build into a bigger piece of finished work but also to encourage playfulness, which involved the informal recording of ideas and thoughts. It was Adrian's reflective approach to working alongside children and staff, gently prompting and questioning more deeply that greatly appealed to me.

As well as being a Year 3 teacher Emma is responsible for the implementation of Assessing Pupil Progress (APP) so it made sense for her to work with Adrian as a way of extending this area of her practice. It was her first experience of working with a creative practitioner and her involvement in each step of the project was crucial to its success as it gave her an equal voice in the direction and the success of the project.

As a teacher what would you need to put in place or to know about to feel you could have an equal say in a project such as this?

## What did we do? The *Northern Lights* project

### Adrian Higgins

We started with a backstage visit to the Birmingham Rep Theatre (www. birmingham-rep.co.uk) to see how their production of Philip Pullman's *Northern Lights* was conceived, produced and staged. The tour had a real 'wow' factor to it. Walking around we saw how a whole host of people with different skills worked in partnership. We saw a creative process in action. Costume departments were littered with sketch books and rough designs; the prop department had half finished ideas strewn across the floor and hung up on the walls; set designers were busy scratching heads and building things. By the time we arrived on stage we had all begun to make meaningful connections between the show and the creative endeavour that sat backstage.

It felt to me as if 'backstage' was where the real learning was going on and so Emma and I wanted the emphasis for the project to be more 'backstage' (process) than 'on stage' (product).

As a way of placing high value on the creative process I introduced the children to my sketchbook practice. It is a place in which I am able to record ideas and experiences. It is a place for me to experiment and try out. It is also a place in which I am able to reflect on how my ideas are progressing and connecting. I ask myself 'What is working? What isn't working? Why isn't it working? What do I need to do next?'

In the context of a school this sketch book practice is a little bit like a learning journal or process diary. Emma gave the children one each. They took them to the Rep and they were to hand throughout the whole project. This reflective approach to learning was different from Emma's existing teaching style and became a feature of the partnership.

The performance of *Northern Lights* and the back stage trip were inspiring and we were left with a raft of ideas to explore.

Emma and I then had a half day planning. It was an opportunity to discuss the different approaches to our professions but we also found similarities and made connections. We agreed that being creative was a learning process and that this was the common ground we should explore.

Planning was large scale, colourful and messy. We decided not to have fixed and immovable learning objectives but instead we would prioritise and make explicit certain criteria in the sessions with the children.

The criteria were:

- identify and promote good creative attributes. 'What helps me be creative?';
- engage children in different forms of writing;
- explore a variety of visual arts media to express ideas;
- develop a reflective practice to teaching and learning.

We wanted the children to shape and have ownership of their learning experience, to be more independent of the teacher and work collaboratively with each other. Emma was keen not to contrive curriculum coverage but instead map out where the children had been and what had been covered at the end of the project. She also kept a journal. The project lasted six whole day sessions, once a week with an evaluation day at the end.

What seemed to really excite the children about *Northern Lights* was the idea of another world beyond theirs and a sense of magic.

What was exciting for Emma and me was that we were about to do something that was less predictable and had an element of risk. We agreed to stand back as much as we could. We decided to put the children on an imaginary island with no grown-ups allowed.

What's your and your school's attitude to risk taking? What's the difference between recklessness and purposeful risk taking? To what extent is risk taking necessary for new ways of working? Who gives permission to take risks in your schools and what happens when things fail?

## Provocation

Emma identified a space that could be used consistently, a regular meeting place that wasn't the classroom. In this cleared room we placed a large flat hessian parcel, with a letter on top in the shape of a boat. We invited the children in to the room and to sit in a circle round the parcel.

Initially the children didn't say anything and were reluctant to speak. Emma was aware that many of her children could be passive and would wait to be 'spoon fed' ideas. I asked them 'Who has got an idea?'

Gradually questions were raised. What could it be? Where has it come from? Who left it? Why was it there? Should I open it? Asking questions and negotiating a way forward was a real challenge. What did become apparent was the children had already placed value on the contents 'Be careful!', 'Don't rip it', 'This is something precious, something different'.

The letter was opened and read out by one confident and curious little girl. It was an invitation on to an uninhabited island. In the parcel was a huge map. It

**Figure 1.1**  A provocation

**Figure 1.2** Design stages from idea to finished shield

was featureless but was divided into four areas. Each area had a further envelope attached to it. These envelopes contained information about the type of community each group would form. There would be a group of witches and wizards, a group of super heroes, some princes and princesses and an ancient tribe living amongst rogue dinosaurs. The children's first challenge was to draw or 'map out' their community. They mind-mapped ideas about dwellings, transport, landscape and work in their journals. The island started to come alive and continued to grow over the next few sessions.

The only interventions that Emma and I made in the first session were either to encourage the children to think and behave imaginatively or to ask questions that would enable each group to work co-operatively. The children realised how the chaotic nature of their behaviour was stopping each group from working effectively. Emma asked them to negotiate some rules that accounted for taking turns when it came to speaking, listening and sharing ideas. The reflective session at the end of the day allowed children to share how they had solved their problems (or not) and share their ideas about their community. On the surface these unusual communities may seem banal but we wanted them to develop because they are the kind of archetypes and characters that children explore outside the classroom. They do this in their own time and in lots of different ways. Children have a lot to say about them; they are relevant and meaningful to them.

Emma noticed how the children had time to get lost and immerse themselves in their ideas. These were whole day sessions uninterrupted and free from curriculum routine.

How important to the success of this project is open ended time? How do you feel about children being allowed to 'get lost' during an activity? Is it necessary to proper exploration and immersion or is the job of a teacher to keep children focused? Does an artist see this differently? What value might this bring?

In establishing these communities the children began to naturally explore cultural identity. One aspect that particularly excited them was their island homes. I introduced them to some printmaking techniques and also some images of different dwellings from around the world. 'What was similar and what was different?' Why do they look the way they do? What is their function?' The children designed and experimented with their own ideas in their journals. They then went on to make a Poly-print of their own dwelling.

The exploration of their identity was a recurring theme in the following sessions. The process through which they took themselves was also repeated – sketchbook work, discussion, refining, developing ideas and then some more doing. There were lots of periods of just talking. One assumption when working creatively is that it is all doing. There is in fact lots of reflection and hard thinking.

Emma applied this refining process to writing. The children wanted to design a badge or motif for their community. She asked them to think of all the things that made their community unique. These words were written down at first spontaneously but then prioritised down to the five most important.

Each word was then represented with a simple graphic. Some of these graphics were then combined to create a badge. This refining process whether with words or drawings was evidenced in their journals. The journal was a learning tool that connected what Emma was doing as a teacher and what I was doing as an artist.

Emma and I consulted with the children at the end of each session about how they might like to explore any emerging themes or interests. Our approach to planning had to be very flexible in contrast to the prescriptive framework that the school was used to. This model allowed the children to retain ownership over their ideas and shape the course of their learning experience.

This flexibility was tested when the children became interested in what they might look like on the island. The children's solution was to dress up so we agreed that they could wear costumes only when the group was together and engaged in island activity. Emma gave them their homework – design and make a costume. It was a task that each child eagerly continued outside school.

Emma and I wanted to explore some of the writing by creating a myth.

Through creating their island the children had already got a couple of key components. Their fictitious selves could be the heroes and the island a possible setting. What was needed now were the other key ingredients. There are five or six elements that make up most popular mythical stories (think of *Jason and the Argonauts*, *Shrek* and *Doctor Who*). I suppose if a myth were a cake then each element would be an ingredient that made up the recipe. I came up with a recipe as follows:

- 1 freshly picked hero or heroine
- 1 home grown companion
- 1 slimy mythical creature (de-scaled)
- 1 massive problem
- A cup full of magic
- 1 difficult journey

**Figure 1.3** Island design

**Figure 1.4** Collaborative designers at work

The big question was what kind of problem were the children going to have to solve? Emma and I stole the map. Hanging in its place was a message. 'Down through the ceiling and on to the floor. I've stolen your map! What next lies in store?' There were also some unusual giant sized foot prints made from flour, a stack of table and chairs leading to a hole in the ceiling and rumbling thunder that played over the school tannoy system. After the initial shock the children became police investigators, observing the scene, asking questions and looking out for suspects. It was an experience they were fully immersed in. It was an incident that the whole school was talking about.

The children then did a number of things.

They made suspects out of plasticine and mind-mapped their suspects, wondering why their map had been taken? They created 'Wanted' posters. They also made a mock up of a stage that reflected where their suspect lived.

So that was their quest. Undertake a dangerous journey, confront your suspect and retrieve the map. Now most heroes and heroines have some kind of magical object or power that helps them in their quest. Luke Skywalker has his light sabre and Wonder Women has her bullet-deflecting bracelets.

The children were given household objects that they imaginatively endowed with magic. They recorded all of this in their journals. They were ready to set off. They were

**Figure 1.5**  A suspect

ready to write. The children plotted out their ideas to include all the key ingredients of their myth and then sequenced the story. Once the stories had been written the real map also returned to school, delivered from the airport with a lost property ticket attached to it. The children were relieved that it hadn't left the country and were bursting with all sorts of new questions. But, we had run out of time.

We wanted the evaluation process to be as creative as the sessions. Emma and I talked to the children about what was different about the sessions and what they thought they had learnt along the way. They then took these comments and together with observations, photos, planning, artefacts and writing put together another scrapbook that reflected their learning journey. We also collaborated to curate a show of their work for a Creative Partnerships event for teachers. I wanted the children to reflect both process and product, drawing on all the tools and materials they had used and produced such as their journals. Once the show was ready the children guided teachers from other schools around their work. They were able to tell them not only *what* they had learnt but *how* they had learnt it.

## What was learnt?

## Emma Davies

The importance of this piece of work for the school has been profound in two respects

### Engaging children in decision making

The change in attitudes to learning is the most powerful message of the project – for me and the children. Although we were tracking carefully the children's attainment I had not considered the power of children themselves as active partners in making choices about what they were going to learn and how they would construct their learning for themselves. What this project made me realise was that for each session, although the initial stimulus would be planned and possible steps along the way mapped out, the children would create the actual reality of their story world for themselves. As each session progressed, Adrian and I discussed the learning so far and planned the next one on the basis of the children's ideas, suggestions and reflections using the learning journals as prompts along the way.

### Evidencing improvement in attainment

We felt it essential to track closely the impact on children's attainment, in this case on writing. Given the needs of the school to focus on attainment in core areas we did not choose to assess the children against any sort of scale for 'creative skills' or 'creativity' simply because, to us, creative skills are good learning skills.

All of the children made expected and beyond expected progress in their core writing skills and we looked in particular at the attainment of the 11 children mentioned above as underachieving.

By the end of Year 3 and three months on from the end of the project nine out of the 11 children had attained more than the expected level of 3 points of progress with the average point increase of the group as 5.6. Interestingly, the whole class made better than expected progress – the average point score increase for the whole class was 4.9. This, I believe, is because the 'buzz' and motivation of the project and in particular of the 11 more able children spread across the class and, indeed, across the school as teachers and children wanted to know what was going on in Year 3 and, equally, as Year 3 were keen to share their ideas with everyone!

Do you agree with this – are creative skills the same as good learning skills? Is it important to understand the gains in creative skills and how would you go about this? Are their reflections the same ones you draw from this project? What other insights can you draw into ways to engage children in learning?

## Conclusion

This has been an important part of the growth of the school along a two-fold path – being absolutely rigorous about tracking the children's progress according to core standards of attainment so that we can fight our corner against external accountability systems, together with developing the freedom for children to dream and to be curious and follow trails of thought into actions.

## Resources

The resources required for this project are set out in Table 1.1.

## Questions for further discussion

1. To what extent are the challenges that Allens Croft face similar to yours? Where are the areas of resonance and dissonance?
2. What did this case study make you think about in relation to your own practice?
3. Adrian made extensive use of sketchbooks to encourage children to record their creative process and reflect on their learning. How do you promote reflective practice in the classroom and what might the use of journals offer?
4. What did skills, practices and ideas did Adrian bring to the project? What opportunities are there to involve creative practitioners and cultural organisations in teaching and learning in your school?
5. What did Emma bring to the partnership? What is needed – both practical and philosophical – to create a successful partnership that impacts on learning?
6. What would you need to put in place to develop similar practice in your classroom – curriculum, time, resources, planning and people?

**Table 1.1**   Project resources

| PEOPLE | FINANCES |
|---|---|
| Head teacher<br>Creative agent<br>Teacher<br>Visual artists<br>Birmingham REP education staff and backstage staff<br>Office staff to book transport and arrange permissions | c. £5,000 for creative agent, visual artist, transport, theatre tickets<br>Art materials<br>Journals |
| **STAFF TIME** | **CHANGES TO SCHOOL ROUTINE** |
| Release time for teacher to plan before the project<br>Evaluation and reflection time between sessions and at the end of the project<br>Time to curate exhibition<br>Head teacher and creative agent planning time | Collapsed timetable for 8 days<br>Additional Space in school required |
| **OTHER RESOURCES** | |
| N. Meager (2006) *Creativity and Culture: Art Projects for Primary Schools*, NSEAD Publications<br>This book helped Adrian to shape some of the sessions and in particular think about how establishing fictitious communities can help children explore real life issues and cultural identity. | |

## 2

# Active approaches to teaching

## Improving and enriching performance and understanding of Shakespeare

Emily Smart and Kat Vincent,

Brannel High School

## Editor's introduction

This case study focuses on the importance of teachers developing a creative pedagogy that motivates young people in ideas and subjects that are challenging and complex. The example from Brannel School near St Austell, Cornwall focuses on Shakespeare but it applies to other subjects and texts that can be seen as 'distant and boring'. The elements of their challenge can be characterised as:

- the pressure to increase attainment;
- the need to develop pupil meaning and connection to learning;
- the desire to develop a 'learning partnership' between teacher and learner;
- the need to develop a new repertoire of teaching skills;
- the aspiration to develop children's 'well-being' and promote collective working.

The development of the teachers' skills and confidence has been achieved through their participation in the Learning and Performance Network (LPN) with the Royal Shakespeare Company (RSC) and the University of Warwick.[1] This case study focuses on the outcomes of this partnership in the classroom.

## Who's who?

- *Emily Smart* head of Drama, Brannel School
- *Kat Vincent* English teacher, Brannel School
- *Practitioners from the Royal Shakespeare Company Education Department* (www.rsc.org.uk) *and academic staff from the Institute of Education, University of Warwick* (http://www2.warwick.ac.uk/)

## The school context and key issues

## Emily Smart and Kat Vincent

- *Name* Brannel School, a Specialist College for English and the Performing Arts
- *Location* St Austell, Cornwall
- *Age range* 11–16
- *No. on roll* 704
- *Website* www.brannel.cornwall.sch.uk

Brannel School believes in the importance of the arts as a means of empowering young people. It is a small rural school that serves the villages in the china clay mining district in mid-Cornwall and its main priority is raising the self-esteem, expectations and attainment of the pupils and families of the local community.

English is a strong department in the school and is part of the specialist status with the Performing Arts. The department have been incredibly supportive of the idea of teaching Shakespeare actively and we feel we have a creative, dynamic and flexible team who are prepared to take risks and try out new approaches. Drama is a valued subject in the school and is taught as a discrete subject for one hour a week throughout Key Stage 3 and has a healthy uptake at Key Stage 4. The exam results have never exceeded 69 per cent of pupils gaining an A* – C in Drama which is not always reflective of the standard of work produced within the department lower down the school. When it comes to preparing for GCSE performance examinations in drama, the majority of students favour working on scripted pieces rather than creating devised pieces and show a lack of confidence in the creative process.

## The challenge of Shakespeare

'Shakespeare may be the most famous author who ever lived, but thousands of children are shunning the Bard because schools are failing to bring his work to life.' So writes Graeme Paton.[2] Is this a sweeping statement or a real problem within our classrooms?

The catalyst for our work together was joining the RSC's Learning and Performance Network. The driver for the network is the RSC's 'Stand Up for Shakespeare' manifesto – 'start Shakespeare at an earlier age, do it on your feet and see Shakespeare live' – which sets out to transform the teaching of Shakespeare in schools across the country. The LPN involves extensive training in using 'active approaches' in the classroom inspired by the RSC rehearsal room, teacher action research and then young people creating performances for a Shakespeare festival.

One of the more rewarding aspects was the opportunity to work together, to collaborate, to share practice and assimilate knowledge. The mutual support was important. One of us was interested in using drama in English teaching towards a written coursework piece and the other was interested in ensemble-based learning and rehearsal room techniques, to boost attainment in Drama. Both of us wanted to connect with students, learn with them, and allow them to experience Shakespeare in a productive and exciting way. This repositioning of the teacher is crucial for pupils to be informed participants in the process of their own learning and because the work is shared and collaborative we were hoping it would create a creative learning partnership between young people and adults.

> How often do you get the chance to work collaboratively with colleagues on an innovation in school? Having a partner to share success and failure with is an important aspect of this case study.

The involvement with the RSC clarified what we wanted for our students and boosted our confidence to change the way in which Shakespeare is taught and the whole ethos surrounding students' response to Shakespeare. At the beginning of our three year journey, the majority of student responses would have been negative: 'Shakespeare is boring. I don't get the language. It's frustrating'. Below we describe our different experiences of teaching Shakespeare and how we both achieved 'creative classrooms'.

## Timeline

- *2007* Brannel School join the LPN.
- *2007– 2008* Kat involved in five days' training with RSC/Warwick in active approaches to teaching Shakespeare in English and undertook an accredited action research project.
- *2008–2009* Both Emily and Kat involved in five days' training with RSC/ Warwick practitioners in active approaches to teaching Shakespeare in Drama and undertook an accredited action research project during the year.
- *January–March 2009* Both Emily and Kat's classes rehearse and perform a scene at a Shakespeare Performance Festival along with their local primary schools.

## Case study 1: Year 10 Drama

## Emily Smart

I had begun the school year with a challenging GCSE Yr 10 group and progress was hampered by poor behaviour, a lack of confidence and an unwillingness to commit to practical work. I was interested in how ensemble learning could shape confidence and achievement in an exam-focused setting by concentrating on the process of creating a performance. I also wanted to examine attitudes to Shakespeare, who was a playwright I had tended to avoid, preferring the security of other tried and tested GCSE texts.

Is this an attitude that you recognise towards Shakespeare and other similar complex texts? What challenges does that bring to you as a teacher?

Over three months, using two hours of lesson time a week, our task was to rehearse the tavern scene in *Henry V* (act 2 scene 1) to perform as part of a local schools' festival. The aim was to use the original Shakespeare text and through a collaborative process build an original piece of theatre. Before the project I expected that ensemble, collaborative ways of working would be challenging but ultimately beneficial to the drama group. We had four support workshops from RSC artists, two of which were designed specifically for the pupils.

My group was made up of four boys and 11 girls of varied backgrounds and abilities. Over 50 per cent of the group had chosen not to be involved in any performance work since entering the school at aged 11, yet they had opted to do a subject 40 per cent of which is assessed on performance skills. I was conscious that I was taking a risk as I was in a sense forcing their involvement in this project. I knew I needed to forge a trusting creative partnership that would allow me to step back and put the young people in a position where they all felt they had a stake.

**Figure 2.1**  Ensemble planning

How do you get the right balance of teacher as guide and pupils taking the lead? It is interesting that Emily uses the phrase 'felt they had a stake' – what are the boundaries of giving pupils choice?

## Building the ensemble

Building the 'ensemble' became essential to breaking down resistance and developing mutual trust. By ensemble I mean working collaboratively instead of working as a group of 'individuals'. We spent a month working on ensemble exercises with the purpose of including everybody. Despite the improved group dynamic, the effect was short lived and it was only when I introduced the text that I began to see development. I focused on the theme of war and the background story of *Henry V*; I kept the facts simple. I told the group that they were going to do a scene set in a pub and prepared some visuals from the graphic novel series of Shakespeare plays (see resources section) adding a caption which summarised the action. I placed them around the room and insisted pupils walk around in silence looking at them, choosing one image/caption and then using the whole group to recreate the chosen moment. One pupil chose the scene of carnage at the end of the battle of Agincourt and he modelled his classmates into an abstract image of the dead amongst the living as the peace settlement was drawn up. It was impressive to observe this pupil leading the group through his idea and for them to respond so readily to his vision. I felt encouraged by the collaborative spirit in the group this engagement had begun to foster and began to see the whole class as a resource, which was changing the way I viewed them.

## Physical actions and ownership

The group's first workshop with a practitioner from the RSC allowed us breathing space. They talked honestly about the barriers they were still putting up, which I felt masked their insecurities about the project.

By the afternoon session, they began delving into character work and by building on their own discoveries the work began to take off. The workshop was structured to give them ownership. Their ideas were developed and theirs was a shared experience which brought obvious enjoyment and a sense of satisfaction. The session had ended with a mini performance of their scene in mime and movement based on the underworld of the low-life characters. One of the boys who had admitted at the start that he was largely unmotivated by Shakespeare had been a major contributor to the workshop. His focus was good and his commitment clear. Peer teaching had been a part of the process and when teaching other groups their moves, this particular pupil had enjoyed the responsibility.

Watching from the outside had given me an opportunity to observe the group and reflect on my practice. It was clear I needed to be more honest and to discuss the frustrations I had with them.

How often do you get the opportunity to observe your pupils at work and the space to relate to your teaching? What happens when you do? Emily's action research project gave her a focus and reason to ask these searching questions.

During each session they initially struggled with whole group tasks and the ingrained low-level disruption was difficult to break down. However, the physical work needed to make the performance had enough challenge for them to respond to and I saw an improvement in attitude. With two weeks of the project left, I read their drama diaries and realised I had begun to find far more opportunities for them to have a stake in what they were learning.

The group had shown genuine interest in finding out more about the characters in *Henry V* and had began to question how they might be relevant to their own lives. One girl commented that she felt the play would appeal to young people because 'they would find it interesting how much Henry grows up when he knows he has to go to war' (Year 10 pupil).

It was the power of the ensemble[3] that allowed confidence to grow. Interviewed afterwards, one girl commented; 'Our groups like really small, and when we've come together, everyone says their confidence has been built up and when we work together we're all like really confident. We're better because we all do it together'. They felt included. Almost all pupils linked positive emotions to the idea of the ensemble; it is 'when everyone feels happy', it is 'about making new friends', about 'creating something magnificent'. For many, it was the collaboration that made the project special.

The development of pupils' confidence is attributed to the power of the social relationships built up through ensemble ways of working in a drama studio or a non-conventional classroom. What might this offer to teachers working to change the generally non-social, individualised 'conventional' classrooms?

As March approached we needed to work from the script. When assigning parts, the group nominated who they felt deserved the main speaking roles in a responsible, caring way. One of the pupils astounded me by his determination to work through his own chronic lack of confidence when reading. When we started rehearsals he clearly struggled, particularly stumbling over 'Base tike, call'st thou me host'. We began trying out different approaches physically, walking in and saying it, tapping him on the shoulder and saying it, running in and shouting it. I suggested cutting the line, but the boys insisted we continue. Finally we tried an arm wrestle and this action of pushing and resistance helped him get a sense of the physical demands of the text and he began to make sense of it.

This boy made meaning of a complex text through physical action to connect to the character he was playing, which mirrors the creative process that actors go through. What might this process of physical exploration offer to learners making sense of difficult concepts and ideas?

Many began to express a far more positive attitude towards the project; all seemed to thrive on the collaborative element of the project and regularly took pride in 'the group';

> I'm happy about doing it. Miss always asks if everyone feels confident and at first we all said no, but now we're all confident. It's just like the more you do, the more you learn about it. For a while you just get into it. You realise you're not scared.[4]

The group remained committed to rehearsals and proudly performed their *Henry V*. The work on Shakespeare had allowed a sharing of responsibilities and it had united people. On the night of the performance, I felt the final piece was almost insignificant compared to the unified spirit of the group, and that was very much their victory. A post project questionnaire revealed that everyone felt an improved teacher and pupil relationship and effort and achievement grades had all risen. Ninety-two per cent enjoyed the performance, 78 per cent felt that they would get involved in another school production, 65 per cent feel more likely to devise their own piece for their forthcoming exam.

## Case study 2: Year 10 English

## Kat Vincent

I was the first member of staff to embark on RSC training and remember coming back to school feeling enthused, wanting to share what I had learnt, but concerned – I was coming back to a small classroom in rural Cornwall where I knew that attitudes to Shakespeare amongst the students were quite negative. I realised quite quickly that it was possible to teach actively in a small space and the need for a more active approach was essential in order for my students to gain a wider 'experience' of Shakespeare.

## Teaching *Othello*

My first experiences of working actively were with a top set Year 10 class. For me, the reasons behind changing my practice with this particular class were simple: they weren't enjoying Shakespeare as much as I expected them to. I became very aware of their acceptance of simply sitting down with a text and reading through it and I found it dulled the meaning of the text, made lessons predictable and gave far less meaning to the words. If I felt this as a teacher, I wonder how they must have felt. It was comfortable, safe and familiar – but was it *interesting*?

Gibson (1998b) recognises that 'teachers' attitudes are crucial – teachers who are enthusiastic about their subject, and who teach in interesting ways, motivate their students to share that enthusiasm'. I had to remain focused and enjoy the first couple of active lessons in order to not let the class know this was 'new ground' for me. As the project progressed, I was far happier to let the classes know that we were trying something new together, as I felt more confident that they accepted I was having a go at something different. This made them feel valued, that I cared enough to try something new.

What did I hope to see? For me, the most important part went back to the RSC principle of creating an 'ensemble' in the classroom – the notion of all the students in my class working together to create a purposeful, comfortable but challenging environment in which everyone is engaged and has a positive learning experience through active drama approaches. From a personal perspective, I wanted to improve my own confidence in teaching Shakespeare in an active way – challenging myself to try new methods in the classroom and stepping out of my own comfort zone to join the pupils in a creative partnership. Lastly I was very aware that I needed an end product: a GCSE coursework essay that reflected their learning experience. I hoped that by using drama methods, the students would create a well informed and in depth coursework essay, which reflected their own interpretations rather than being 'spoon fed' the interpretations of others.

I was made aware of the gamble I was taking by a well meaning member of staff, who brought it to my attention that I was 'risk taking' with a top set GCSE class who were already performing well. Trying a different method of teaching with a class already performing well *is* taking a risk. What if they just sat there? What if they said no? What if no one in the class offered to perform or show anything they had done? I realise now that these thoughts were really just

**Figure 2.2** Exploring *Othello* in an active way

my way of coping with the fact I had to be well planned and confident in front of my class, for if I faltered and they realised that I was lacking in confidence with the methods I was using, they would not embrace what I was asking them to do.

What are the risks and rewards of sharing your insecurities with your class? How does this affect power relationships? Is it possible to develop new practice *without* admitting you are taking a risk? What was the most important factor in convincing Kat to take the risk?

I decided to try a brand new text and *Othello* was chosen partly because no one in the department had taught it at GCSE before, and also because it is a text that dealt in universals – betrayal, jealousy, race, multiculturalism and power. This was my first challenge as it is a play that I was only vaguely familiar with, and one which I hoped I could develop a scheme of work from as the work progressed. I did not 'formalise' the scheme of work I intended to teach, but altered and adapted it depending on what was successful and what wasn't. In this way, the scheme of work itself became cyclical, with improvements and additions along the way. Lots of the active approaches were taken from literature I had read (particular note here must go to Rex Gibson's 'Teaching Shakespeare', see resources section) and some approaches I created myself, or developed from ensemble techniques I had experienced in the rehearsal room.

## Creating an ensemble, consolidating new pedagogy

The RSC advocate that teaching Shakespeare using drama is about creating an ensemble – but nowhere does it tell you how long you have to wait before you actually recognise one within your own classroom. I wasn't sure whether my class would co-operate with each other, so it came as quite a surprise to me that on only the second lesson in the scheme of work, when I ran a 'whoosh' on *Othello* (a rapid, active way of condensing a play into an hour, where all students are involved in creating the scenes) that the students really seemed to gel with each other. They were encouraging of each other, openly laughing and having fun, and challenging themselves a little. There were still those who found it a little uncomfortable, but their peers were listening and mature. I found I was left with a spare ten minutes at the end of the lesson, and 'off the cuff' decided to ask the students to take a section of the play that they found interesting and produce a tableau, a still picture using their bodies like a photograph. The class organised their own groups and produced some amazing tableau work with very little encouragement or guidance from me. This quickly became one of their favourite ways of showing their interpretations and as a starter activity to recap plot and during plenary when discussing character motivation and intent.

## Improving teacher confidence

My confidence improved during the project, so much so that I will never revert to teaching Shakespeare without active approaches again. The high point was during a 'teacher in role' activity early on in the delivery. I had seen an RSC practitioner perform 'in role' and wanted to challenge myself to do it, so I took on the role of the Venetian Senate, questioning Othello about his relationship with Desdemona in Act 1 scene 3. The students played the combined role of Othello, and I asked them questions to help unravel the language and make sense of a long speech. I had seen this technique, known as 'interpolated questioning'[5] used without notes from a confident professional, but as I had not attempted it before, I drafted the speech on paper and this worked really well as the 'senator' looked impressive in his gown and his roll of parchment (with all the questions written on). It was a high point because students fully believed the scenario we had created and it helped unlock meaning – they said 'it makes the speech make sense when you put those questions in'.

Both teacher and pupils are involved in 'purposeful play' here. Where are the opportunities for you to encourage similar purposeful play in your practice?

Language use is one of the more difficult aspects of teaching Shakespeare's work, often causing students' to become convinced that they don't understand what's going on. Because this strategy had worked so well, they were more able also to grasp the rhythm of the Iambic pentameter and how it was used in Othello's speech to make him seem calm, reserved and noble.

Results taken from a class questionnaire for my research show a positive significant shift in thinking. Over the period where we had worked as an active classroom, the students became more confident and competent in using and understanding Shakespeare's language.

I realised quite quickly that 'risk taking' shouldn't be considered as risky. If, as teachers, we want to remain fresh and dynamic in the way that we deliver our curriculum there are options available to us if we are prepared to invest our time and energies into making changes. Once I'd started teaching actively, the way I felt about teaching Shakespeare changed. I looked forward to the lessons and there was a 'buzz' in the classroom that is difficult to quantify but whenever we created something together it made a difference to the way I was feeling and the way the students were responding.

## Transferring active work to paper

The prospect of writing an essay after so much active input was daunting: students are used to having written notes and resource sheets available so there needs to be a balanced relationship between this and the drama work for them to get most benefit. I created guidance notes about the activities to help them recall what we had done. The essays I received showed success – students produced technical and demanding essays with the majority achieving As or A*s. It is difficult to predict what results I would have achieved using my original teaching method, as I had no 'control' class as a comparison, but this is the highest set of coursework grades that this class had produced as a whole during the 12 months I had been teaching them. More importantly for me, the students' perceptions were altered:

> Active methods are more fun and engaging, meaning we pay more attention. Furthermore, as we act and explore the language we can see, from a different point of view, how language, actions and staging is used.

> If you get the right guidance with the active work you can suddenly understand it. You have to listen to get it. It puts loads across in a different way.[6]

The students link their engagement in their work (listening, paying more attention) to the form of teaching they have received. From these examples, how would you describe that pedagogy?

## Changing futures – teaching differently and learning actively

### Emily Smart and Kat Vincent

The emphasis on ensemble working was challenging to both groups but it has benefited them all; it has 'made things happen' for them in a more significant way than we first thought. This project proves that that there is a clear link to the development of students' social and communication skills once they have discussed, performed and collaborated. It is the experience of being part of this project that counts, the early process of building the ensemble, the process of exploring the scene and characters.

Our relationships with both groups are vastly improved. We are more pro-active at stepping back and allowing them to ask questions and to let the work take on new aspects and move in a direction dictated by them and their learning needs.

The work on Shakespeare has helped to unlock student's resistance and helped them understand the responsibilities they have towards each other, the school and even the wider community. As practitioners, we want our experiences to become collective knowledge that others can draw on and use to become more confident with using active approaches in the classroom and studio.

In picking up GCSE work in Drama after the Shakespeare project, students used rehearsal time more purposefully on text-based tasks. There was increased support for each other and more willingness to experiment with scripts instead of hiding behind them. There seemed to be less bravado, less joking, less of a 'let's make it funny' attitude moving from stereotype to a deeper understanding of characterisation. They had realised that a more serious approach meant they could be truer to the character they were playing. There has been a definite shift towards devising theatre pieces, rather than 'hiding' behind existing scripts. Over half the group have created their own pieces for their performance exam which is a truly impressive development. In English we continue using dramatic approaches to text-based work, becoming increasingly more exploratory. Learning 'on their feet' enables pupils to keep hold of their creativity and dramatic connection to the play even though they still have to formalise their work in an assignment. Although it now seems obvious, we have almost merged the two departments together in the way that we teach Shakespeare – one question we often ponder is why it took us so long to find common ground in our approaches.

## Resources

The resources required for this project are set out in Table 2.1.

**Table 2.1**   Project resources

| PEOPLE | RESOURCES/ FINANCES |
|---|---|
| English teacher (and wider departmental colleagues)<br>Drama teacher<br>Deputy head teacher as SMT Champion<br>RSC practitioners<br>University of Warwick staff | Contribution towards participation in the LPN<br>Cover for training days<br>Minimal props and costumes |
| STAFF TIME | CHANGES TO SCHOOL ROUTINES |
| Release time for teachers to attend RSC training days in Stratford and with local cluster of schools<br>Planning time to organise festival contributions<br>Teachers' own time to undertake study and action research project and plan new schemes of work<br>Evaluation and reflection time with RSC practitioners visiting school | Re-arranging English classroom – pushing the desks back |
| OTHER RESOURCES | |
| DSCF (2008) *The National Strategy; Shakespeare for All Ages and Stages*<br>R. Gibson (1998) *Teaching Shakespeare,* Cambridge University Press;<br>J. McDonald (2007) *Henry V – the Graphic Novel,* Classical Comics Ltd;<br>J. Stredder (2004) *The North Face of Shakespeare; Activities for Teaching the Plays,* Wincot Press | |

## Questions for further discussion

1. The authors describe the challenge of leading a creative process that is working towards an end product, in this case an essay or a performance, which serves as a means of summative assessment. Should we assess creativity in classrooms by the quality of the process or by the actual creative achievement that results? Who makes those assessments? What criteria should be used?

2. This case study draws on the expert knowledge that the authors have gained through an action research process and commitment to sharing their learning. In undertaking a similar professional development programme how might you structure such an inquiry and who would you share it with?

3. The authors emphasise the importance of building a classroom ensemble as a condition that enabled students to explore Shakespeare in an open, collaborative way. How does this challenge the image of the individual creative genius and how might that be useful to you?

4. This case study illustrates what teaching for creativity can look like with a real emphasis on partnership working: between student and teacher; between teachers; between departments. What opportunities exist in your school to develop this? Where is the urgent need in your school and who are the people with energy and motivation to work with?

5. This example shows the importance of incremental development to introducing new creative practice. As the teachers' confidence grew, new possibilities emerged and the concept of what was risky to them expanded. What are the potential rewards and punishments for taking a risk to teaching practice in your school? Is there a difference between your tolerance to risk and that of the organisation? What would be required to create a more risk-friendly environment?

**3**

# Ensuring equality with a focus on boys' learning

Lorna Rose and Angela Carlin, Lillian de Lissa
Nursery School and Children's Centre

## Editor's introduction

This case study shows how the philosophy and working practices of Lillian de Lissa Nursery School were applied to the issue of boys' development and how this led to curriculum innovation and ongoing staff development. The authors illustrate this through a number of examples and highlight the role of creative practitioners.

The elements of their challenge can be characterised as:

- a concern about boys making slower progress than girls;
- the need to understand why this was so;
- the need to develop a curriculum and activities that might address this;
- the need to introduce more male practitioners into the nursery.

This case study also highlights that the creative and imaginative growth of children should be part of a child's everyday experience rather than confined to individual projects.

## Who's who?

- *Angela Carlin* deputy head teacher
- *Lorna Rose* artist in residence
- *Matt Shaw* creative practitioner
- *John Godbold* creative practitioner
- *Ros Bayley* education consultant

## The school context and key issues

- *Name* Lillian de Lissa Nursery School
- *Location* Birmingham
- *Age range* 3–4
- *No. on roll* 78
- *Website* www.ldelissa.bham.sch.uk

Lillian de Lissa Nursery School, part of Lillian de Lissa and Belgravia Children's Centre, is close to Birmingham city centre and has a transient population made up of families from many cultural and linguistic backgrounds. Eighty-eight per cent of our children are from an ethnic minority background, including several newly arrived families; over 40 per cent of children have English as an additional language and come from a range of diverse backgrounds using up to 20 different languages. In order for all children to be successful it is vital that we are in tune with our children and families many of whom have pressing economic needs and difficulties in managing everyday life. The nursery is able to draw on the rich mix of cultural resources from both immigrant and more established families which the children bring with them to school.

Using the children's ideas is strongly connected to promoting their well-being and value of their own cultures, whilst also challenging them to extend thought and knowledge. The school's goal is to provide an appropriate and fully inclusive range of opportunities. The overarching ethos is aimed at providing the environment and support in which children can be curious, make significant discoveries and mistakes, and enjoy learning about the world we live in, whilst building positive relationships with others, children and adults.

## Timeline

- *September 2009* Ros Bayley runs whole day staff training about the differences in girls and boys' cognitive development and implications for different types of learners.
- *November 2009* Our pupil, Ali takes part in Forest School for six consecutive Fridays.
- *January 2010* Ali involved in whole school peer massage and working with engineer Matt Shaw, who is in school one day a week for 12 weeks.
- *January 2010* Storyteller John Godbold works with the boys for 24 days over the Spring and Summer terms.
- *April 2010* New and larger materials with unusual and dynamic properties are introduced into the school environment.

**Figure 3.1**   Absorbed in a task

## The school's principles and daily ways of working

Our style of education has expanded over 15 years of training and staff professional development. This has included study tours researching early years provision in Reggio Emilia in Italy, the Forest Schools of Denmark and the Swedish education system. They all share our belief that every child is born with immense potential and that through play and curiosity children can construct and communicate their own learning journey.

We set out below the insights from this research on our practice.

The first is the centrality of reflective practice, which is observation, interpretation, action and observation. This is a cycle of watching how a stimulus is used by a child, thinking about and discussing what learning is taking place and how it can be extended. This can lead to a deeper level of understanding about a child's learning and enables effective extension of interests and projects. During daily 'walkabout' meetings after school, we discuss the happenings of the day which are recorded and become the planning for the next day's provision. Reflection with the children happens at group times each day where they are asked about what they want to do, what they have done, are able to look at photos and can discuss their thoughts about their play.

'The 100 Languages of Children' statement (also a touring exhibition and a book from Reggio Children http://zerosei.comune.re.it/inter/100exhibit.htm)

reminds us that children communicate with us in a huge range of ways, not just verbally. This encourages us to act upon the diverse range of learning styles and follow child-initiated ideas however bizarre they may seem.

The environment is the third teacher; the first being the child and the second the practitioner. This approach to teaching puts the natural development of children and the relationships they have with their environment at the centre of its philosophy, involving children making their own choices of materials and how to use them.

Is it possible or desirable to plan for learning in the way the authors describe beyond the early years? What are the challenges to practice of listening to children and genuinely following their interests?

## Making the best place to learn

Over the years we have considered what makes the best place for children to learn and develop. The challenge is to make these ideas real in everyday practice and was one we faced anew when setting out our enquiry into how we could improve the outcomes for our boys. We think it is useful here to set out the foundations we had already established in our practice before we illustrate how we approached developing our provision for boys.

## Partnerships between teachers and creative practitioners

Our analysis of our discussions, photographs and videos show that there is a different kind of relationship formed between a child and creative practitioner. Creative practitioners have a different agenda and set of expectations which are strongly focused on generating and exploring ideas, following them through and communicating them. Many of the creative practitioners we work with support the children to make exhibitions, performances and displays which show the results of the thinking and doing that have occurred.

## The environment

This is an essential aspect of enabling children to explore and discover solutions within a creative framework, developing learning and thinking through multi-sensory experiences. We saw that in Sweden and Denmark the outside space is used every day, whatever the weather. The focus is also on play such as collecting natural materials, growing plants, building dens/shelters and experiencing camp fires. As a result we have established a 'free flow' nursery where children can choose where they want to be, work and play. The outside area is available at all times and the resources in and outside are updated and changed regularly and are accessible to all children.

## Motivation for learning

This is generated through communicating with the children about what they would like to explore. We use an approach where we show pictures of each area in school and the possibilities explained, linked to a specific practitioner, type of materials or theme. Each child then chooses what they want to do.

## Attending to the whole child

We encourage personal, social and emotional wellbeing through the regular use of yoga, peer massage, cookery, therapeutic music, nurture groups and visits to local amenities such as galleries, parks and shops of interest. We aim to provide a holistic education and give our children a good grounding in how to behave in a considered manner in a variety of situations and environments.

## Listening

Listening to and observing the children are vital to personalising learning. Looking at where the children like to play, listening to the dialogue used and being aware of the social dynamics is vital to extending their play. As the needs of our children are different every year, the daily routine is tailored to suit the changing dynamics. The process that we use is one of daily pedagogic observation so planning is a process of observing children's responses to each day's provocations, reflecting on these as a team, and then deciding how to extend the learning.

How would you summarise the principles and philosophy of learning in your school or setting? How do they inform daily practice? What's the place of creativity in your curriculum?

## Developing provision for boys

In 2009 we noticed that the boys came out as less developed than girls when we combined the results of our Early Years and Foundation Stage (EYFS) assessment of all children with our observation records. We noticed the following:

- linguistics – boys use fewer words in their play;
- physicality – boys prefer active pursuits in every area of learning;
- large-scale play – boys are more inclined to take on challenges and take risks;
- shorter concentration time – boys showed less ability to sustain activities.

We knew that this was not unique to our location but we had to find ways of addressing the issue that were compatible with our ways of working. As a whole staff we engaged in professional conversations about these concerns for boys' development. We suspected that:

43

**Figure 3.2** Joyful play

- the type of resources and environment might significantly enhance the attraction to boys and therefore the likelihood of their interaction and engagement;
- inviting male figures into school might provide role models and opportunities for discussion;
- supporting and praising the boys differently from the girls may extend interest in a subject and encourage further investigation.

To extend our thinking we worked with Ros Bayley, a freelance educational consultant who explored with us the findings of her recent publication *The Cleverness of Boys* (2010). She suggests that boys and girls do not learn in the same way because boys have lower 'boredom thresholds' so it is essential to give them frequent breaks and opportunities for movement. After a day of working with Ros we concluded that we needed to be particularly aware of the following factors in our practice with boys:

- use simple clear instructions and repeat them several times over;
- boys need to move more so do as much outdoor learning as possible;
- plan for the fact that boys need more space for learning, indoors and outside;
- praise and recognise boys' abilities to think in the abstract;
- help boys to work in groups with sensitive support.

While these generalisations are useful in focussing on the key issues, observation is the key element in choosing the most appropriate learning methods for each child, so it was also important to work with boys individually, allow for their differences and not just see them as being the same. We decided on an action research approach that combined acting on our hunches about what might make a difference, with close observation to provide evidence of progress so we could adjust the activities for each boy.

Do you recognise this analysis of development issues for boys and the school's subsequent hypothesis that inform their planning? What else would you add or challenge?

## Developing the work with boys

An example of how the staff responded to these ideas was during the 2009 school year when we developed activities arising from the boys' play in school such as their super hero play. We observed that many of the boys were very interested in play fighting and killing which is very normal in boys of this age. This raised the question of 'how could we give these children a wider vision of the real danger of guns and the finality of death?' After staff discussion it was agreed that through support and dialogue the play would be angled to address the fact that once someone was 'dead' the game was over. Our focus was on the process of adventure that was happening and the 'super powers' that most cartoon characters have. We encouraged the boys to concentrate on rescuing and planning rather than have the adventures come to an end. We used the boys' ideas and channelled them, rather than ban their games altogether.

Most of the teaching staff at Lillian de Lissa is female so there is a natural confidence about what the girls are interested in but not necessarily what the boys like. One response to this is to have male practitioners in school on a regular basis to inspire and provide positive role models for all of the children but boys in particular. These creative practitioners are here throughout the school year and often for a whole term. The examples we share below illustrate different examples of practice involving male practitioners, what they brought into school and what resulted.

For most of the 2009/10 school year we have been working with storyteller John Godbold. We have observed him build a positive relationship with our children by using stories that many of them are familiar with, such as *Billy Goats Gruff* and *Goldilocks and the Three Bears*. First, he tells the story, and then encourages them to change and make the stories into their own creations. He works by providing a provocation for the children to respond to – a hat, a bridge, a book with empty pages – and then uses all of their ideas as part of the ongoing adventure. His skill and speed of collating group stories, and the physical nature of his style of practice has made him a success with the children, particularly the boys who talk about working with John on a daily basis and are very enthusiastic in developing their stories to share with him. John then produces the children's illustrated stories so they can be read and used as a library resource and we have seen that free access to self-generated stories re-confirms the children's

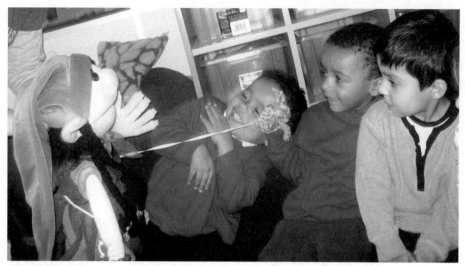

**Figure 3.3** Story making with John

ownership of the work. This has proven to be a successful tool in raising self-esteem and confidence levels which is shown by the children's feedback during reflective sessions.

This work confirmed our speculations about what might be required to better engage boys and we looked at how to bring together the insights from our creative practitioners with our ongoing daily activity. One specific example of this is with Jack, a child who has an interest in all living things. He was in his element during his Forest School sessions and has continued to follow this interest in all areas of the nursery by looking at books related to animals, searching for insects, using the school grounds to their fullest extent and playing with, researching and talking about dinosaurs. This personal interest makes him very knowledgeable on this subject and able to talk to children and adults confidently, with skill and accuracy. His passion has been shared with his family group and there was much child interaction around the subject of dinosaurs. Our challenge was to extend and develop this interest in a meaningful way. When discussing Jack's interest with the staff team, several possibilities for learning extension were considered such as visiting a local geology museum to see fossils or building his own dinosaur in the art studio.

To develop these ideas, sand and mud were put in a large tray for Jack and his friends to investigate and from this play he began to create characters and a narrative in describing his actions. During one of John Godbold's visits Jack shared his knowledge with him and John then began to construct a new story investigation that included all of the children in the nursery. The new story involved a man-sized dinosaur called 'Terry Rex' who came to school for a day, joining the children for group time, eating lunch and playing alongside the children. For Jack, this reinforced that we valued his knowledge and boosted his self-esteem and confidence.

The role of documentation and staff discussion was critical to understanding Jack's interests and thus engage him in meaningful activities. What opportunities are there to work in this way with a much larger ratio of adults to children? What might that mean for the way in which different professionals work together?

## Ali's story

We focus here on the story of Ali. Ali was a very quiet child who lacked confidence but had made a significant friendship with one child in the nursery setting. He was reluctant to initiate his own learning and stuck with relatively simple activities such as playing in the water or sand trays. It was noted that he was unsteady on his feet and didn't move with coordination and control. He seemed uncomfortable in an active environment and didn't move freely with the pleasure or confidence the EYFS Framework suggested he should be able to at his developmental stage. Whilst observing Ali during six consecutive weeks of Forest School in our local woodland area, it was noted that he found it difficult to work with the other five children and lacked self-reliance and self-esteem. As a staff team we designed a two stage project to encourage him to join in with other children and gain self-belief.

First of all we encouraged Ali to work with creative practitioner Matt Shaw who runs projects based on engineering and design tasks. The aim of the project was to challenge both staff and children to extend the range of materials we use and to provide possibilities of physicality within learning. The activities mainly took place outside in the school grounds and to begin with, focused on weird and wonderful large scale building materials and functional objects that Matt brought with him. The children were invited to play, explore and instigate ways of working with this collection of unfamiliar things.

After a number of sessions watching the other children work with Matt, Ali chose to investigate the large scale pipes and crates. He approached this in a considered and deliberate way and seemed to enjoy doing so. Ali lined up a set of crates and then began to insert pipes in the gaps between the crates. He did this without assistance and maintained his focus for a long period of time. He appeared to have developed a plan for this activity. This was a dramatic change to his normal style of working because these actions were self-initiated, sustained and generated a visible enthusiasm. He was energetic and attempted physical tasks that he ordinarily would not have done.

The teacher supporting him observed his interaction at a distance but stayed nearby to give him encouragement. Photographs were taken in order to note the environment and atmosphere that had stimulated this type of play, so that we might learn how to extend his interests and learning further. We decided that during the following weeks the same materials would be made available to him alongside different objects for him to include in his play. He worked well with the objects familiar to him and became open to introducing new elements at his own pace. This was the first time that we had observed Ali responding to materials (a stimulus) at this level, setting his own agenda and sustaining interest.

**Figure 3.4** Construction

We then decided to re-make the situation to inspire Ali in the indoor environment using similar types of materials but on a smaller scale. Tubes, ramps and mini-crates were provided which quickly became marble runs for the other children while Ali watched. After a few days he began to join in, following his own interests and skills. We observed that Ali was more confident and relaxed around nursery and more motivated to explore new opportunities. He began to access the art studio more regularly and respond to subjects in media new to him (like chalk, pastels, ink). We felt sure that this was directly connected to working with Matt and using the relatively unusual materials in the outside project.

Our Deputy Head Teacher had recently taken part in some training and thought that 'peer massage' might be a tool to enable his interaction further. Peer massage was introduced by each group's key worker to all of the children in school. Having to ask a partner if it is OK to touch them and then go on to apply appropriate pressure to make the massage effective and enjoyable requires communication and consideration which the children had to learn. Ali was receptive and enjoyed this activity as we hoped he would, and a daily massage session went on to reinforce and develop his relationships with the other children.

What skills were being developed by Ali in his play with the materials? In what sense might they be described as creative skills?

## Additional actions

In the first year of our action research we have implemented two new initiatives designed for all of our children, but particularly to support the needs of boys.

We have formed nurture groups which are small groups of children – three or four, working with the same adult each time in a safe and comfortable environment. The children involved have to make their own rules of 'how to be in the group' and are all given a chance to speak and be listened to during the routine meetings together to focus on a specific subject. The same children meet until the staff member running the group feels that a change is needed due to progression, dynamics or any other contributing factor. This strategy addresses the ongoing concerns about emotional and social development of young children and in time, can create a bond, greater knowledge, confidence and trust for those lacking in communication and social skills.

The Social Use of Language Programme (SULP) (http://www.wendyrinaldi. com/) is an initiative to support appropriate social interaction and a child's learning within a group. With four trained staff members who run the programme in school, this is a framework which develops children's interpersonal and social abilities from a communication and thinking skills perspective. This is achieved by using games, activities and discussion about listening, taking turns and having respect for each other. The SULP initiative is encouraged to continue within the classroom and involves a reward system of stickers to celebrate achievement.

We have now added to this, Every Child A Talker (ECAT)[1] to promote and encourage the use of speech and language. This is a two year national project involving parents and children, looking at the importance of talking to babies and young children in order to build a foundation for learning and life skills. We feel that gaining the skills to understand, respond and communicate at an early stage in life enables a child to embrace the enjoyment of learning.

## Conclusion

As a result of our attention to the equality of provision over the last two years we know that greater development is being shown in the Communication, Language and Literacy area of the EYFS guidelines. Our statistics confirm there has been an increase in boys attaining the age related band in this area. At the end of the school year 2008/2009 10 per cent of boys were in band 6 for this area but this year there has been an increase to 17 per cent. We believe the significance of this improvement to be directly related to the appropriate creative initiatives put in place during the school year.

Our boys are telling more stories, showing developments in both language and imaginary play. They are still not picking up commercial books in any great number, but this may yet come when they want to work with different stories and themes. Our documentation evidences how this provision has helped to motivate and inspire the children and the decisions they make in directing their own learning. These 'soft' outcomes show children's deeper level learning and can go on to help produce 'hard' outcomes as they go through the education system. We cannot imagine returning to a situation where children are not engaged in creative approaches to learning and to a school which does not have a mix of teachers and creative practitioners.

## Resources

The resources required for this project are set out in Table 3.1.

**Table 3.1** Project resources

| PEOPLE | FINANCES |
|---|---|
| Angela Carlin, deputy head holding the curriculum overview<br>Lorna Rose, artist in residence, coordinating external practitioners<br>Creative practitioners and artists sourced through research and contacts | Artists were paid £200 per day through funding from the nursery's core budget and from specific initiatives like Creative Partnerships and local arts/education projects<br>Use of CPD budget for whole staff training<br>Recording equipment – cameras and video for documentation<br>Journals and books to hold documentation on each child |
| STAFF TIME | CHANGES TO SCHOOL ROUTINES |
| Time for planning and reflection after school<br>Joint planning and evaluation between staff and creative practitioners | Minimal – the most significant changes is now embedded when we moved to become a 'free flow' nursery in 2006. Staff followed children rather than the other way around |
| OTHER RESOURCES | |
| S. Featherstone and R. Bayley, (2010) *The Cleverness of Boys*. Early Years Library, Featherstone | |

## Questions for further discussion

1. The image of the child that the nursery promotes is the touchstone for their practice. What is the image of the child that your school promotes and to what extent does it inform your planning? What are your beliefs and values?
2. The school places high value on the development of the imagination and of children's creativity. To what extent is this a romantic notion which has to be tempered with a focus on knowledge and 'hard' outcomes as children progress through school?
3. Over time the nursery has developed an ongoing 'plan to plan' which enables it to respond immediately to children's interests and to the unexpected. What benefits might this offer to you and where might you begin? Is this even possible?
4. While Lillian de Lissa trust their own documentation to evidence children's progress, they also use the EYFS for external accountability. Do the frameworks you use account for creative development? If not how would you describe them? Does this term mean the same thing at early years compared to higher up the school system?

5. What do you take from the nursery's analysis and response to the issues they saw in their provision for boys? Are there common principles across boys of all ages?

6. The head teacher and governors of Lillian de Lissa have chosen to use the budget to employ creative practitioners instead of other support staff due to the value they see them bring. What would be needed to create the evidence base in your school to make such choices?

# 4

# The neighbourhood classroom

Jeremy Brown and Gill Hutchinson,
Deansfield Community School

## Editor's introduction

This case study documents how Deansfield Community School has looked to their neighbourhood as a resource for creative learning and a 'real world' context that will generate relevance and meaning for its pupils. In looking outwards young people encounter and work with adults from different professions and roles, so widening their understanding of the world and life beyond school. The example here looks at young people as researchers and consultants on a controversial housing scheme and raises ethical questions about the right role for young people in this process. The elements of their challenge can be characterised as:

- the pressure to raise attainment and meet pupil progress targets;
- the need to find the hooks and triggers to excite children in Key Stage 3;
- a desire to create 'authentic learning' models;
- the focus on developing individual and team skills as much as knowledge.

  This case study shows how after eight years of practice engaging with the local neighbourhood is embedded into the thinking and planning of the school. It also shows that by going out into their locality and connecting with people that live in it and manage it, those people are now coming back into school which keeps the potential of the neighbourhood as classroom alive and sustainable.

## Who's who?

- *Jeremy Brown* creative agent
- *Matthew Buckham* Midland Heart Housing Association
- *Rachel Dickins* deputy head teacher
- *Gill Hutchinson* community development consultant
- *Kenny Aitchison* Wolverhampton City Council

## The school context and key issues

### Jeremy Brown

- *Name* Deansfield Community School
- *Location* Wolverhampton
- *Age range* 11–19
- *No. on roll* 698

Deansfield Community School has used its School of Creativity status to push learning beyond the classroom. It began with an opportunity to use the city council's local housing programme as a context through which we could explore settlement in Geography and has evolved to embrace intergenerational activity with the school's wider community.

The school serves a mixed catchment on the edges of Wolverhampton city centre. It consists of established local families who tend to have low levels of academic qualification and a high percentage of students with special needs and a growing number for whom English is a second language (2009's figures showed 30 per cent of pupils on the SEN register, 15 per cent with English as an additional language). The school has had to work hard to improve attainment which has been achieved in part through the introduction of different qualifications which contribute to GCSE scores. Vocational courses are popular with our students and with recent changes at Key Stage 3 we have introduced a curriculum designed to develop pupil's Personal Learning and Thinking Skills (PLTS).[1] The same school coordinator and creative agent have guided Deansfield's participation in the Creative Partnerships programme since 2002, coinciding with an increase in students achieving five A*–C grades at GCSE from 19 per cent to 73 per cent.

> The continuity and drive of the leadership to develop creativity in school is a vital part of Deansfield's story. Who would you need to work with to play a similar role and who might be a senior champion in the school?

The school recently chose to introduce an ASDAN (http://www.asdan.org.uk/) Qualification in Citizenship (which contributes towards GCSE scores) in Year 9 to extend opportunities for independent project-based learning. This is taught in blocks and fits neatly with our ambition of creative learning projects which require extended time and an engagement with the locality.

As part of the school's commitment to pupil voice there have been high profile opportunities for students to comment on and shape school life such as the organisation of the school day and improving teaching and learning. For instance, the school pioneered 'Have your Say Days' using a series of video booths accessible to all students. These activities, along with extensive feedback from previous Creative Partnerships projects emphasised the value students attach to working with external partners.

## Our approach to making creative partnerships

Given the circumstances of the school our challenge has been to ensure impact on pupil attainment and progression. The pressure to attain over 30 per cent GCSE passes in Maths and English is a priority, but there is also a genuine commitment to making learning relevant and embracing external opportunities which inspire and motivate students.

The support from the senior leadership team means that teaching staff are encouraged to embrace flexible approaches to timetabling and accommodate requests for groups and individuals to come off timetable for project activity. This creates tensions at Key Stage 4 and we try to keep all key staff fully aware of plans from the earliest stages. Creative Partnerships activity in various guises is flagged up in weekly diary sheets, at staff briefing twice a week and at whole school staff sessions every Monday. After eight years the approach has influenced teaching in all subject areas, is a regular agenda item at governors' meetings and is embedded in and beyond classroom practice.

When we create a partnership or a project we use the following factors to guide our planning once the leadership team and creative agent have identified themes for teaching and learning which have the potential to impact on standards, set out in Table 4.1.

Do you find these criteria helpful? What else would you add into a list of factors to consider for planning for partnership projects in your setting?

## Working in the local neighbourhood and influencing regeneration

Our initial involvement with regeneration began in 2003, when the school was in the centre of a radical housing scheme. This was virtually opposite the school site and impacted on the lives of our students. Several families were 'decanted' or forced to move and large scale demolition meant the route to school was fractured by a derelict 12-acre site which was soon fenced off and secured.

After conversations with pupils we saw this as an opportunity to explore a very real and immediate context for teaching. It was evident that local families were not fully aware of what was happening; there had been some consultation but this had not involved many of the people who were now in the midst of major change and

**Table 4.1**  Creative project planning considerations

| DEFINITION OF CREATIVITY | PUPIL VOICE |
|---|---|
| Our definition of a creative practitioner has moved beyond the traditional artist in residence to embrace a wide range of well qualified professionals who use creative thinking in their working lives. | Projects are developed with students who input ideas, agree milestones and outcomes. Pupils like working towards a well defined outcome which brings with it urgency and deadlines to engage them in the project. Opportunities for showcasing and celebrating outcomes give the work a high profile and allow parents and families to share in their children's achievements. |
| NEW SITES FOR LEARNING | SKILL DEVELOPMENT |
| Projects are designed to engage all students by making learning relevant and challenging. Night clubs, building sites, shopping centres, galleries, football stadiums and the local airport have all been used as classrooms where teachers and other professionals have delivered imaginative cross curricular work. | We want to develop students' transferable skills so engineer chances for them to meet professionals who apply a range of skills in their work. This provides a broad interpretation of 'creative industries' and extends to both public and private sectors. |
| REAL WORLD PARTNERSHIPS | GROWING OUR AMBITION/SECURING RESOURCES |
| Many of these projects are supported by local private sector partners; the school has built up long term links with retailers and cultural organisations including the local gallery, theatre and media centre, local authority officers with responsibility for PR, planning and design and a number of developers, contractors and housing associations. We use these to make learning relevant – we ask can the students relate to the learning? Will it interest them? Will it 'hook' them in? | This approach requires buy in from staff, a range of partners and the capacity to support and run ambitious programmes. Our response has been to raise significant additional support, both financial and in kind using Creative Partnerships funding as leverage to draw down further resources. This has enabled us to develop a progressive model of entitlement which seeks to ensure all year groups participate. |
| CROSS CURRICULAR CONNECTIONS | SUSTAINABILITY |
| Making connections across subject areas reinforces learning. It also offers the chance for colleagues that might not normally get the opportunity to collaborate to work together. | We think about how far we might repeat the project or develop the partnership. How might we make this an expectation of the students and school life and maximise the potential of the creative idea? Could other colleagues or other schools use the idea? |

**Figure 4.1** The neighbourhood classroom

upheaval. As a conduit for getting information back to parents and other adults we recognised that the students could have a role to play.

The creative agent initiated meetings with the City Council's Planning Department and involved teaching staff from different departments including humanities and art and design.

Officers from neighbourhood renewal and regeneration volunteered to come and speak to groups of students at school. John Brothers from the local authority who was overseeing the regeneration commented:

> I learnt more about the regeneration issues facing the community during an hour's session with the pupils than in a week of reading reports. Regeneration discussions are often professionals talking to professionals, children rarely play a part, although arguably their views are the most important. They are the people destined to inherit these neighbourhoods.

Deansfield was recognised as the ideal focal point for activities to allow local families to become involved and shape the planning processes which were going to have a direct impact on their quality of life.

With guidance from officers involved in neighbourhood renewal the staff developed a wide ranging programme which included an interface with designers and architects and extensive collaboration with the appointed developers. A core group of teaching staff explored how a 12-acre brown field site could be used to deliver themed teaching opportunities as the site was gradually transformed over a three year timescale. A plethora of projects emerged such as creating show homes, consulting with residents and presenting to the planning committee, historical and archival projects capturing life in the 1950s on the estate and a Year 10 group worked with a sculptor to design fencing panels and gates celebrating the local flora and fauna as part of a public art commission.

The project brought with it an unprecedented level of public interest and was followed by regional and national recognition for the school, the city and for the developer, Persimmon Homes. This was instrumental in rebuilding the confidence of the local community after a challenging period at the end of the 1990s when the school was required to rapidly improve after an external inspection.[2] This newly found outward facing character was to be a key feature of the new school culture.

> What are the local issues that impact on your pupils' lives and what opportunities are there for engaging with those that are shaping these issues? What other curricular opportunities might there be in such projects?

The example we profile here is with Midland Heart Housing Association who approached the school in the summer of 2009. They had bought a derelict pub site near the school to develop as 'Move On' accommodation for young people aged 16–25 who need support to live independently. This had been met with opposition from residents who had campaigned through the local press on community safety concerns which had prompted Midland Heart to re-think the plans and propose a general use housing development. As part of this re-think the school agreed to take on a potentially controversial community consultation led by Year 9 as part of their ASDAN course.

The residents 'not in my back yard' stance over supporting a minority groups was further aggravated by misinformation and rumour. Our previous work had convinced the city council that by using students to gauge local opinion there would be wider ranging and more honest results. We saw this as an opportunity for students to prepare and develop an authentic piece of local research accountable to an external client and an ideal way for pupils to develop and practise creative skills.

To ensure pupils had the right skills we employed Gill Hutchinson, a freelance consultant who had previously worked with us on the integration of economic migrants in school and has an outstanding track record in consultation and conflict resolution. Gill specialises in working with community groups across the country and uses techniques designed to encourage active participation in local issues. She brings with her a great experience coupled with an infectious enthusiasm for her work. Gill expertly models the skills and behaviours we want for our students such as problem solving and communication. As a successful freelance consultant she demonstrates considerable expertise in organisational skills and project management, which qualifies her as an ideal practitioner to work with some of our more challenging students. They respond well to her no-nonsense expectations and are caught up in her passion to tease out and resolve complex affairs.

The deputy head teacher worked with the creative agent to map out an eight week project. Gill planned a detailed schedule of work with the creative agent, class teacher and Midland Heart that would meet the ASDAN assessment criteria. This included research methods, gathering and evaluating data and using ICT to present a report. The group of 26, Year 9 students had chosen this course and had not worked together before; they included a range of abilities and some students were known to be harder to engage and motivate.

The school was also able to call upon expertise from the local authority, Midland Heart Housing Association and their chosen architects so giving more opportunities for students to engage with a number of professionals.

## What did we do?

### Gill Hutchinson

I feel passionately about ensuring that people have an opportunity to influence and effect change in the neighbourhoods where they live. I use visual and creative techniques to engage with people and have built up a varied 'toolkit' to share with young people. The main concerns for me in this project were to ensure that the group had an opportunity to plan, deliver and take ownership of it. I wanted to encourage them to try different approaches and to develop their creative thinking ability to imagine and propose new solutions.

During my first contact with the group I was struck by the variety of personalities; some were very confident whilst others were reticent and unsure of what was expected of them and whether they would enjoy this project. At least two members of the group were not team players and insisted on working alone. I realised it was going to be a challenge to manage this group; we had a lot of ground to cover in the six days allocated for the work. I was allotted a day a week to work with the class so I needed to ensure that I provided enough stimulation to keep them fully engaged throughout the day.

Initial discussion with the class centred on their understanding of a community which began with them describing their own experience of belonging. Many of the group were fiercely territorial, with limited experience of regional travel but they also showed a tremendous curiosity for what made places safer or more attractive. Their family ties were significant in restricting mobility and a majority expected to be living in the same area for the foreseeable future. We used examples from other areas to expand our thinking such as an anti-social behaviour incident in Leicestershire which had resulted in the death of a mother and daughter. This led into a discussion around being a good neighbour and citizen with reference to personal safety and behaviour.

Kenny Aitchison, the Principal Development Officer (PDO) at Wolverhampton City Council talked to us about the history of social housing, the current housing shortage in the city and the challenges of developing housing projects for vulnerable people. We encouraged pupils to think about their aspirations for where and how they expected to be living in the future.

During these discussions Kenny talked about the difficulties of housing young people who had encountered complications in their lives, particularly through their involvement in crime or drug misuse. Some of our students were affronted that adults did not want them living close by or felt that they would cause problems to other residents. They were appalled that communities would try to stop accommodation that would enable young people to get their lives back on track.

This project was rooted in consideration of citizenship and questions that affect our society and the way we live. How important do you think it is that the ethical and moral dimensions need to be explored, as well as the technical course requirements? How did the real life nature of the project enhance this? Can you think of a comparable opportunity in your locality?

The following week involved officers from Midland Heart Housing Association and the architect of the proposed development. This gave the students experience of working with creative professionals and a chance to understand the revised plans more fully and why they had changed. The discussion moved into the unexpected but relevant territory of entitlements for single parents and the space they thought a young mother would need to be able to look after a baby.

In week three the group started to plan the consultation exercise beginning with a visit to the site to see first hand where and what it was. They needed to think about the make up of the area – what type of people lived on this estate? Was there any evidence of who lived here? What evidence was there to suggest that older people may live there? Were there many people walking around the estate or did it appear that most people were out at work? I also asked the class to look for evidence of any problems including untidy gardens, broken fences, graffiti, burnt out cars, fly tipping and other damage.

The next thing to consider was where the consultation could take place. We spoke to local shops, the library and the local primary school where a 'school gate' activity was planned to take place when parents and carers were picking up their children. This was a very simple exercise but the group became very excited with the status they gained from taking on a professional task; they looked at familiar sites and buildings through new eyes and came away with useful evidence.

When the pupils arrived back at school after the site visit they planned their research. They were asked to build up a profile of the ages and gender of people living in the area, the type of tenure of the property they lived in and some general information about how they felt about the East Park area. In addition they were asked to create a range of images for the large visual questionnaires that would be used at the school gates and in other public places. They tested their questionnaires on members of staff and older students and I briefed them about staying safe whilst they were interviewing on the doorstep and we agreed how they would introduce themselves. They then spent a day interviewing residents on their doorstep and approached people in the street. A small group of young people volunteered to consult with parents and carers at the school gates using the large visual questionnaires.

**Figure 4.2** Out and about

It became evident that residents were concerned about the revised plans for developing the site with many believing it was still to be used for 'Move On' accommodation. Many believed the development would house ex-prisoners who were convicted paedophiles or were drug addicts. Whilst the young people tried to explain that the plans had changed many residents didn't believe them and some thought Midland Heart were using the students to persuade them. In addition some residents approached the class teacher on the street to express their concerns and, in one case, 'disgust' that the young people were not in school learning.

The class had very mixed feelings about the information they were gathering. It was evident that some were very touched by the concerns of elderly residents and the fear that had been generated. They were upset that some residents had been in support of the initial plans but were too frightened to admit this at the public meeting and felt intimidated by their neighbours. They also felt a sense of frustration that they weren't believed about the changes to the scheme because they were young, and were angry that some residents felt that learning could only be achieved in the classroom. Many indicated that they had learnt a lot from talking to people in the street or on the doorstep as some of the older people had talked about their lives and experiences of living on the estate. Many of the class live on the estate but hearing other people's views made them realise how they are affected by anti-social behaviour. The group also acknowledged that at times they had found it hard to listen to derogatory views without expressing their own opinions.

During the consultation I felt a great sense of pride in the way the class conducted themselves. Approaching people in the street or knocking on doors to survey residents requires confidence and good interpersonal skills. The young people rose to the challenge and conducted themselves in a professional manner. They came back glowing with positive stories and conversations; Jack met a Spitfire pilot from the Second World War; Olivia spoke to a woman who had been at Deansfield School 40 years ago and reminisced about her teachers. It became apparent that the dynamics of the group were changing. The quieter members of the group appeared to participate more readily and the two group members who wanted to work alone had gradually started to work more closely with others. Within days of the consultation exercise press releases appeared in the local paper highlighting residents' concerns about the new proposals and a further public meeting was organised, which the pupils didn't attend. It was apparent that residents believed Midland Heart were using the young people to misinform them.

The situation had to be managed very carefully. Jeremy and I had to think about whether it could be perceived that the young people had been manipulated.

How would you defend this accusation of children being manipulated? What would your response be? Is this a valid criticism?

However we believe this project provided the opportunity to engage with a community who could be termed as 'hard to reach' or seldom heard. Like many pieces of work involving communities things don't always work to plan, and you have to be able to deal effectively with the unexpected, which with our support the young people were able to do. The research challenged the group to think on their feet and adapt what they were doing; trying different approaches and framing questions depending on the responses of interviewees. I believe this encouraged them to think creatively and not be frightened to change a plan of action as the need demanded. We felt that young people had to understand what was happening and to think about the role and power of the media. They grasped that in this situation the media had helped to frighten and misinform local people resulting in much needed accommodation being scrapped and replaced by flats for people on the housing waiting list.

In total just over 100 people were interviewed and the completed data analysed. A report of the findings was presented by the group to Midland Heart and 12 of them volunteered to present at the Civic Centre to local council members, officers, staff from the housing association and parents and staff from school. The presentation was scripted and rehearsed and backed up with a PowerPoint presentation which included photographs of the group in action along with statistical evidence of their findings.

The presentation led to a lively question and answer session which was facilitated by Jeremy. Officers from local authority and the press asked about the process work and challenged some of the statistics. Both council members in attendance arranged to visit the school and one suggested this was 'the best presentation' he had ever seen delivered by pupils. At the time of writing plans for the site have still to be finalised and the reality of changing timescales and the complexity of planning and financial constraints has not gone unnoticed by the students who are now in Year 10.

The reflection with pupils at the end of the project showed how they thought they had benefited. Many said that they felt their confidence had increased, saying they found it easier to participate in discussions and to express their views. A number of young people welcomed the opportunity to be involved in a 'real' project – a piece of work that was going to be useful to someone. They recognised that the dynamics in the group were constantly changing and the project had provided them with the opportunity to work with different people. The young people were equal contributors to all aspects of the project and thrived on the status and significance of the work they were undertaking. The work had an urgency because of the timescale and this motivated the group – they were 'on a mission' to get the job done.

## Some pupil reflections

Jack: I think this project has helped me gain more confidence – I've had to get out there and learn to speak my mind.

Ali: I have liked the fact we have been allowed out of the classroom into the community to go and learn about people's views on a complicated subject.

Rhys: I liked going out and speaking to loads of different people – I think this has helped me learn more skills in communication and team working.

Jess: I have learnt that people's views affect the way things are done and can change things.

This project has reaffirmed my belief that there is a 'classroom in the neighbourhood'. A neighbourhood provides young people with the opportunity to explore how people live their lives, the pressures they face and to gain an understanding of their variety of views. Some of these views challenge young people to think about their own perceptions and prejudices, how these have been developed and to compare them to those of their peers. It was evident that the neighbourhood classroom provided these young people with an opportunity to thrive and show their capabilities in a way that couldn't be achieved in the traditional classroom setting.

## Legacy

### Jeremy Brown

The legacy of the project has been significant. The recognition the group attracted from staff and parents has raised their sense of their own capabilities and achievements. The group was asked to repeat their presentation as part of a celebration of creative learning at school; this involved parents and families and allowed other staff and members of the local authority to hear about the project.

Midland Heart hosted a visit to a new residential centre in Stafford for the group to meet three homeless people. The students were amazed and moved by the stories they heard from a company director who had struggled with alcoholism, a prospective undergraduate who had left home due to domestic violence and a young ex-offender who was determined to regain access to his 3-year-old daughter. This built on the work with Gill that encouraged a consideration of the causes of homelessness and whether those affected are just as likely to be victims of circumstance. At the start of the visit the class were nervous but began to ask questions and take a genuine interest in the residents, who in turn were fascinated by the attention and were generous with their time. Photographs were taken for the *Midland Heart Newsletter* and we took two of the residents out for lunch with us before returning to school.

Teachers across the school have noticed that the group are more confident in telling us when they are finding work exciting and challenging (or not) and as they move into Year 10 we are continuing to track their progress in research methods and in their speaking and listening skills. The project with Gill provides evidence for their portfolio towards their ASDAN qualification which is expected to be the equivalent of two GCSEs; our assessment shows this project, which makes up a quarter of the total marks, has been extremely successful.

## Resources

The resources required for this project are set out in Table 4.2.

**Table 4.2**  Project resources

| PEOPLE | FINANCES |
|---|---|
| Deputy head teacher<br>Creative agent<br>Class teacher<br>Community engagement practitioner<br>City council and Midland Heart staff | c. £4,000 fees for creative agent and creative practitioner<br>Transport to various locations including the civic centre |
| STAFF TIME | CHANGES TO SCHOOL ROUTINES |
| Release time for teacher to plan before the project<br>Evaluation and reflection time between sessions and at the end of the project<br>Deputy head teacher, class teacher and creative agent planning time | 8 x days out of school during humanities session |

## Questions for further discussion

1. Deansfield place great emphasis on their work having a real world connection. What are the benefits and challenges to pupils of such an approach?
2. Do you agree with Deansfield that the value of creativity is primarily concerned with developing pupil skills?

3. How might your citizenship curriculum be enhanced by connection to your neighbourhood? What kinds of creative skills and behaviours could you develop through this?

4. What would you need to do in order to take advantage of the opportunities?

5. Deansfield are active in promoting and publicising their pupils' achievements. What role do you think recognition plays in motivating pupils? How do you do this in your school and how has this case study made you think differently about this?

# 5

# The place of possibilities

Jane Hanmer, Leighswood Primary School

## Editor's introduction

This case study describes the motivation, process and outcomes of exploiting the potential of outdoor learning to engage and motivate young children. It sets out in stages how a new outdoor space was designed and created and explains the educational philosophy and practice that informed the development. The author is particularly concerned with promoting an active role and voice for children and shares examples of how she used observation as a key tool to achieve this.

The elements of their challenge can be characterised as:

- a concern that children could achieve more, given a better environment;
- how to synthesise new influences and ideas and realise them on the school site;
- how to fuse physical improvement to the site with thinking about ways to teach in them;
- the need to find materials and activities that inspired children's curiosity and progress across all areas of the curriculum;
- how to sustain and develop the completed space.

This case study shows how school can become a place to create community and how parents can be welcomed and engaged in their children's education from the very beginning. The author argues that with a bit of creative thinking and a lot of hard work, any space can offer a plethora of possibilities. It is the approach to creating learning opportunities within the space, combined with the way that children use these opportunities as a springboard for their development that is paramount in developing their learning.

## Who's who?

- *Jane Hanmer* nursery teacher
- *Suzanne Clifton, Sue Lockley, Kim Mole* nursery practitioners
- *Brenda Birch* Children's Centre manager
- *Debbie Banks* Children Centre teacher
- *Jan Taylor* head teacher
- *Claire Witcomb, Karl Lewis* artists

## Timeline

- *June–July 2008* Planning and discussing ideas.
- *September 2008* More planning and discussion with artists.
- *November 2008* Development work began – two days a week.
- *March 2009* Majority of work completed.
- *June 2009* Open day when parents and children helped to complete project.

## The school context and key issues

- *Name* Leighswood Primary School
- *Location* Aldridge, Walsall
- *Age range* 3–11
- *No. on roll* 550

Leighswood is a large primary school located in Aldridge, on the eastern edge of Walsall. Our nursery, which was remodeled in 2005, offers part-time places for up to 78 children. Between the two buildings of Key Stage 1 and Key Stage 2 there is now a new Children's Centre which opened in September 2006. The Children's Centre[1] offers families information on health and social care, as well as wrap around care for three and four year-olds, and before and after school care for five to eleven year-olds.

I have been a teacher at Leighswood for three years and brought to it a passion for creativity and outdoor learning. There are a number of influences on my practice that I was able to combine on the project in this case study:

- My first head teacher made a big impact on me with her passion for 'listening to children'.
- A study tour to the Reggio Emilia pre-schools in Italy in May 2005[2] opened my mind to the use of 'intelligent materials' which provide stimuli to a child's imagination by offering a plethora of open-ended opportunities. I also saw the importance of making children's learning 'visible' by producing documentation of the learning of each child. Children were acting as researchers and the adults were working in partnership with them.
- I worked with artists on a consultation project with children under 5 in order to influence the development of public spaces. The creative practitioners

showed me a new way of seeing things, allowing me to move my focus beyond the curriculum content of a project to a holistic concern for young children. This affirmed my belief that children can have a voice if they are engaged and motivated in their own learning and can see this influence the wider community.

- My own learning journey has continued with the opportunity to become a Forest school leader (http://www.foresteducation.org/) which encompasses all I believe in as an Early Years practitioner. This promotes the personal, social and emotional well-being of children achieved in and through the outdoors.

## Starting out: the stimulus for the project

The staffing and daily timetable of the nursery allowed children the option of being outdoors for most of each session and our observations showed that the majority of our children chose to be outside as much as possible. It was popular but we knew there was more that children could achieve if we had a better, richer space.

Many of the team had visited some amazing outdoor spaces in Danish schools (see http://www.forestschools.com/history-of-forest-schools.php) which had given them first hand evidence that young children achieve optimum development in a rich environment full of possibilities and stimuli. We were excited about the idea of constructing a space that could better engage our children in their learning. We felt this would make a significant contribution to enabling children to achieve their full potential and develop their imaginative play, creativity and thinking skills. We also had a wider concern that as our children's use of the outdoors was diminishing in their time out of school we wanted to ensure that their access to outdoor play was increased within our setting.

For such an ambitious project we chose to work with artists who had worked with us before, shared our educational values and brought a range of art forms and practical skills. Claire Witcomb and Karl Lewis were commissioned to work with us on the process of transforming the outdoor space. Karl and Claire work in a flexible way that enables projects to evolve and they engage children and adults in their design and realisation, which in this case took three months. Their commitment to process allows for things to be re-thought, re-considered and amended as needed. With the team in place we were motivated to be ambitious and the school provided a budget of £20,000 from a combination of sources – Creative Partnerships, the school's own budget and a Big Lottery Fund grant under the Breathing Places scheme (see www.biglotteryfund.org.uk/prog_breathingplaces).

## The development process

We started by creating a brief for the new space through asking questions and involving children in the research. We generated the questions to help us think about the practical realisation of the space and the impact it might have on our own practice, set out in Table 5.1.

**Table 5.1**  Planning questions

How do we guarantee that children have a voice in the decision making?

How might we support all areas of the Early Years and Foundation Stage (EYFS) curriculum in the outdoor environment?

What do we want in the space?

How do we engage with our creative partners?

What might we do to offer our children more physical challenges?

What is the role of the adults?

How do we make decisions?

How do we evaluate any changes to our children's learning?

## Visiting other sites

Next we visited other settings to be inspired by existing good practice and develop practical ideas. We visited Bloomsbury Nursery and Lillian De Lissa Children's Centre, Kingswood Early Years Outdoor Centre, Birmingham Museum and Art Gallery, Cantlop Woods in Shropshire (a private wood used by schools in the area to deliver Forest school projects) and Penn Hall School Special School for 3–19 year-olds that is developing the Forest School approach.[3]

The visit to Cantlop Woods was my first taste of Forest Schools and it took my breath away as I watched three year-old children climb high up the trees. I saw children exploring, balancing, concentrating, creating, questioning, using tools and even cooking marshmallows on the fire. I wanted our children to have this type of amazing opportunity. At Kingswood Centre we saw the use of naturally found materials offering endless possibilities for learning and so we joined the Wolverhampton Forest School Group to share ideas and gain inspiration.

As Claire also worked in Bloomsbury and Lillian De Lissa Nursery schools she arranged for our whole staff team to visit as a group. These settings showed us how much could be done in a limited urban space. They offered a plethora of opportunities for children to initiate their learning whilst supported by enthusiastic adults who adapted the space and materials according to the children's ideas, schemas and approaches.

Where could you look locally for inspiration and ideas for developing your outdoor areas?

These visits inspired a training day for all Foundation staff on 'Why Play Outdoors?' During this session we asked questions about our own childhood, where we played when we were young, what with and why? We found that we had all spent most of our time outside, making perfume from rose petals, mixing mud pies, climbing, using any tools we found and remembered feelings of excitement and tiredness. We shared our experiences from the visits and generated practical actions, such as 'I can look when I'm at the car boot for old kitchen tools, the children would love potato mashers in the mud.'

## Observing children: a tool for gathering information

Observation is much more than writing down what you see a child doing; it is about 'listening' to the child, listening to all their senses, their 'one hundred languages' in the words of Loris Mallaguzzi, one of the founders of the Reggio Emilia pre-schools approach (see Chapter 3 for more details). This is only achievable if the child is viewed as capable and competent, a participant in society and not simply preparing to be so. This view of the child is part of our ethos at Leighswood. We applied the same principles to this project that we would to any action research using a cycle of observations, reflections and action planning. Observations are a normal part of our working day and of each child's 'Learning Journey'. To inform the development of the new space we observed children using the existing space so we could learn about:

- where they played most;
- whether their preference was for big open spaces or the smaller secluded areas;
- what they like to do in these areas;
- the learning opportunities in the different environments.

Our observations used both narrative and photographs with many notes taken 'on the hoof' to capture moments of children's conversation, actions, questions or comments. The following notes were taken at the beginning of the project and highlight how the space was used by a child on her first day.

### Maya's First Day

*Name*: **Maya** (age 3) *Date*: **3.11.08** *Time*: **2.10–2.20**
Maya was outside with her friend Charlie looking in the tyre swing. 'It's not water, it's mud water' she said, trying to tip it out. She struggled to pick the tyre up and could hear Charlie calling her. He had invited her to sit on the back of his bike while he rode it. After riding along the path, Maya said: 'I want to get out now, let's go on something else … you stay on that and I'll go on this', as she sat on a bike. Maya tried to pedal but found it difficult so she got off and shouted to Charlie to come on the climbing frame with her. Maya climbed onto the climbing frame and wanted to go down the fire fighter pole. Charlie said 'I'll show you' as he slid down the pole. 'Mrs Hanmer!' shouted Maya, 'I'm not going unless I get a teacher here' she said to Charlie.

I supported Maya as she slid down the pole. 'Watch out Maya' said Charlie as he climbed down the pole after Maya, 'I'm going to fall on you.' After this Maya and Charlie went back on the bike.

'Don't go really fast' said Maya, as Charlie rode along the path very fast. 'I want to go inside now, Charlie, I'm going inside' she said as she ran across the grass.

However, she changed her mind and went back to the climbing frame, this time going along the top through the tunnel and down the slide.

Then she went back on the bike again, pedalling a short distance before scooting along. She saw Charlie again and got on the back of a bike as if expecting Charlie to get on the front but when he didn't she decided to get on the front and have a go. 'We've got the same' said Charlie.

'No, I've got two whole seats on mine' she said, pointing out the difference between the two bikes.

Maya continued to play with Charlie on the bikes until it was time to go inside.

**Figure 5.1**   Maya and Charlie

## Analysis of observation

Maya showed the confidence to link up with others for support and communicated with me when anxious about her ability to use the apparatus. She was developing and continuing to form friendships that were made in the Children's Centre and communicated her needs and feelings with adults and familiar peers. She showed increased control in gross motor skills when climbing and riding a bike.

Both Maya and Charlie chose physical play, using the bikes and climbing frame. Their physical play was not particularly challenging or risky as they did not move beyond the tarmac area as other areas for physical play were limited and there were no other areas to climb and explore. They did communicate with each other but this was limited to statements rather than conversation. We noted that in three areas of the Early Years and Foundations Stage Framework (EYFS) highlighted in Table 5.2 there was little evidence of progress for Maya. (See http://nationalstrategies. standards.dcsf.gov.uk/earlyyears.)

This kind of analysis focused our thinking on what we might need to do to create opportunities for progress across the whole framework.

## Managing the process

The project was a collaborative process involving many people; children, nursery nurses, teaching assistants, parents, teachers, artists and school management. The team brought a wealth of knowledge and ideas from different viewpoints to extend the vision and possibilities of the design.

For instance those who had been to Denmark brought their photographs and instances of practice that could be useful such as children using tools. Karl offered his ideas and experience on what could practically be achieved in the space and the materials that could be used to do this. For example he suggested we use metal storage boxes as workshop spaces instead of a wooden tool shed as they could be clad to look natural and fit in with the environment. The involvement of the head teacher meant that decisions could be made and costs were carefully controlled and she often found further resources for yet another idea.

Meetings that involved everyone were rare as the two artists worked across the region, so the use of informal satellite meetings became an integral part of the planning process. Whole team meetings were never longer than an hour and satellite meetings were usually 10 to 20 minutes. Sometimes it would be the staff meeting to discuss how to use the outdoor area when it was under construction, but, at other times, myself and Karl and Claire would be discussing on site. The main construction ideas, finance and timings were discussed in whole group meetings and then ongoing issues were ironed out in satellite meetings.

As the teacher responsible for nursery and the person who was using the space every day I was the one who kept others up to date with events, relayed possible ideas and changes from others, and kept senior management informed. Information was shared with Claire and Karl who ultimately were responsible for the design and as trusted partners they were allowed the flexibility to adapt the ideas whilst in the process of construction. The rigour of the planning process helped us to generate and select the most promising solutions.

In a complex multi-partnership project agreeing the processes and protocols for planning and decision making is critical. What seem to you to be the most important factors that need to be agreed?

Table 5.3 illustrates our process for moving from problem to solution.

**Table 5.2** Mapping observation of Maya on the EYFS

| PERSONAL, SOCIAL AND EMOTIONAL DEVELOPMENT | COMMUNICATION, LANGUAGE AND LITERACY | PROBLEM SOLVING, REASONING AND NUMERACY | KNOWLEDGE AND UNDERSTANDING OF THE WORLD | PHYSICAL DEVELOPMENT, MOVEMENT AND SPACE | CREATIVE DEVELOPMENT, RESPONDING TO EXPERIENCES AND EXPRESSING AND COMMUNICATING IDEAS |
|---|---|---|---|---|---|
| • **Dispositions and attitudes**<br>• **Self-confidence and self-esteem**<br>• **Making relationships**<br>• Behaviour and self-control<br>• Self-care<br>• Sense of community | • **Language for communication**<br>• Language for thinking<br>• Linking sounds and letters<br>• Reading<br>• Writing<br>• Handwriting | • Numbers as labels and for counting<br>• Calculating<br>• shape, space and measures | • Exploration and investigation<br>• Designing and making<br>• ICT<br>• Time<br>• Place<br>• Communities | • **Health and bodily awareness**<br>• Using equipment and materials | • Exploring media and materials<br>• Creating music and dance<br>• Developing imagination and imaginative play |

**Bold** indicates areas of progress made by Maya

**Table 5.3**  Planning questions and solutions

| OBSERVATION EVIDENCE | PROVOCATIVE QUESTION | PROPOSED SOLUTIONS |
|---|---|---|
| Pets were a strong influence on the children | Could this develop into an interest in wildlife if we developed some wildlife areas? | Bird hide – children involved in the designing<br>Create a wildlife area and ensure children can access it more often – move existing fence back  (supportive head teacher to pay extra for this ) |
| Physical activity particularly gross motor was important (e.g. Running down the hill) | How could we offer more risk and big physical challenges? | Create more hills and natural climbing areas … but leave spaces they already love such as the long hill |
| Few fine motor skills were occurring outdoors | How would we ensure fine motor skills were developed? | In a workshop shed create a 'magic box' using 'intelligent' or open ended recycled materials for opportunities to make and create, using tools with a direct link to outdoors |
| Wheeled toys were really popular every single day | Do we need more space for wheeled toys? | Leave existing space but provide child accessible storage |
| Role play was related to *big* physical movements e.g. superman | What types of spaces might support other kinds of role play? | Smaller spaces such as willow tunnels, tree house, allotment, sand play, building area, bird hide |

## Children's involvement

In conjunction with our observations, children were consulted about their ideas as we wanted them to participate in the design and physical building of the space. A place was made outside where children were given time and space to draw and talk about what they would like in the nursery garden. They tended to draw what was already in the garden and showed us the features that were important to them in the existing space such as the bikes and the hill. However they also imagined development possibilities such as a campsite, a waterfall, flowers, growing food for Ginger our rabbit, a 'Wacky Warehouse' and a swimming pool. These ideas provided an insight into the types of new features that might inspire them and were taken to the design meetings.

Meaningful rather than superficial consultation with young children presents a challenge. In what ways has the school worked to make this process as genuine as possible? What else might you have done?

**Figure 5.2**   Ideas for the new space

**Figure 5.3**   Detail of design ideas

**Table 5.4**  Initial designs solutions

| SPACE | PURPOSE |
| --- | --- |
| A workshop | A place where children could access tools and a range of natural materials with open ended opportunities |
| A tree house | A place to encourage role play and physical challenges |
| A hill | To extend physical opportunities and change the topography of the outdoor area |
| An allotment area | A place that could encourage both family and community links |
| A wild area | A space to encourage wildlife and plants which would extend children's knowledge and understanding of the natural environment |
| Storage space | A wheeled toy storage area, that would double as an imaginative space but would also allow days without bikes when other physical experiences could be explored |
| Resited digging pit | The current digging pit often flooded and was going to be the new site for the allotment area, a higher piece of land was chosen for the digging pit |
| Planting trees and shrubs and willow | Planting would create special spaces for children to play and hide whilst also encouraging biodiversity |

## Initial design

An initial design was produced by Karl and Claire. Sharing these plans with the children developed into a mini project of 'looking at plans and maps' but it also allowed them a deeper understanding of the plans and a chance for us to incorporate their responses in further drafts of the plan. The initial design solutions are shown in Table 5.4.

## Building begins and the children help us

The work was coordinated and carried out by Karl and Claire and during this phase, which took about eight months, the children and practitioners were constantly invited to have their say on its development. Children were given as much access to the evolving site as was safely possible and here are some of our many observations of the way this engaged them:

Karl had began to make a hill in the garden with several tonnes of soil but this wasn't enough for the children, 'We want it higher' several children commented so Karl ordered more soil and made it higher, so extending the potential of the hill for challenge and play beyond that anticipated by the adults.

We'd seen in our research how real life, meaningful experiences engaged and motivated the children. Freddie worked with tools to make posts to fence off the turf to protect it while it rooted into the soil. Leila, Thomas and Finlay worked out how to fix the string on to the posts. 'Shall we wrap it around? Can we hammer it?' What was the solution? The children were invited to find the answer and it took several attempts and different ideas before we worked it out together, working in partnership.

Children wanted to share in the experience of the building and to make sense of the events. One way that children began to make meaning was to act it out in their play. Here they made their own hill from the surplus turf, creating a miniature world identical to the one emerging around them.

Karl was enthusiastic about the children being practically involved in the project and responded to their interests by encouraging them to sow seeds or build the fence.

## The impact of the finished space

Our observations of the children in the new space provide evidence of their increased use of all the areas and engagement in their learning. During the project Claire worked with the children to develop the wildlife area and extend their interest in animals. She set up an activity in our new workshop to gather their ideas about building a bird hide. Other possibilities in the space began to emerge such as the use of 'intelligent materials' or ones that are open to different uses and possibilities.

The following observation that I recorded demonstrates the use of these materials:

> The children had wanted to climb on the leftover garden pallets. They called them 'ladders'. A pallet and carpet were put on top of one of tyres to link it with two poles, a plank, a wheelbarrow and another pallet by staff who told the children to take care as the wood was rough. The children were all over it for the entire morning; there was much positive interaction and collaborative group play. The fact that the plank was a 'wobbly' meant they were able to develop an even better sense of balance and coordination.

How might you include 'intelligent materials' into your setting? How might you involve children in selecting and choosing these materials and giving those choices about what and how they use them?

As the staff, children and parents worked closely together on this project we all became aware of the types of materials that offer opportunities and exciting challenges. As a collective we then began to source materials for the setting. Our workshop is now full of both natural and man made materials that you may not find in many settings ranging from nuts and bolts, hammers and nails, potato peelers, screwdrivers, wood, leather, wire, metal and seeds. We continue to use local scrappage stores and have now developed our own 'Golden Cave' in a garage space where we collect intelligent materials given to us by local businesses or parents. This enables a key feature of our space – it is not fixed but open to change

**Figure 5.4**   Sowing the grass

**Figure 5.5**   The site develops

in response to ideas and the ideas that get pursued are the ones that interest the children. In reflecting on the value of the project Claire Witcomb reflected:

> The legacy you leave is not just in the way that you work in terms of responding to people, spaces and materials but in the process of changing spaces. It offers the opportunity for children and staff to explore, create and imagine every single day.

## Analysis of observation

We needed to know the difference the project had made to parents and children to assess value and impact. One of the first events we held was an open day for parents to come and experience the space with their children. Next came numerous observations to evaluate the space and find answers to our questions. Are children accessing more areas of learning? Are they being challenged? Does the space offer greater opportunities for self-initiated learning? Has the space lived up to its name a 'Place of Possibilities'?

The text in the box 'A Wriggly Caterpillar' (opposite) is taken from a longer observation and suggests that we have made significant progress.

## Reflecting on learning and development

Phoebe was using tools to plant the sweet peas showing her ability to problem solve when finding a space to plant the peas. Her awareness of space and measure was established as she asked questions on size. Phoebe took the lead in this investigation of the caterpillar. She was always involving Theo in her play and verbally communicating with him expressing ideas, asking questions and giving him information. She displayed high levels of involvement for an extended period of time and encouraged others to be involved, creating a sense of belonging to the school community. Phoebe responded to others' feelings, moving the caterpillar away from children who appeared scared. She demonstrated a sense of caring for others when she moved the caterpillar at Theo's request. Phoebe showed good observation skills when investigating the caterpillar noticing pattern and change in shape. Her creativity was evident when suggesting and designing a house for the caterpillar and her engagement shows how the bio diversity of our garden has led to new possibilities for children.

The highlighted areas in Table 5.5 shows how Phoebe was making progress in all areas of the EYFS, in comparison to the more limited opportunities for Maya in the first sample observation in Table 5.2.

We also wanted to know how parents viewed the space. The way we judged this was by their level of practical support and we found that as they became interested in our garden they sent in spare seeds and plants, offered tools, volunteered to weed and so on. This showed us that we had succeeded in giving ownership to everyone.

### A Wriggly Caterpillar

*Name*: **Phoebe (age 4)** *Date*: **23.04.10** *Time*: **11.20 – 11.40**

Phoebe was busy helping me plant some Sweet Peas in the garden. It took us a while to decide where to plant them. I informed Phoebe that they grow very tall. 'How big?' she asked.

I said I wasn't sure so we looked at the information on the seed packet to see how tall they grew.

We discussed the pros and cons of various sites.

'The bikes will run over them there' said Phoebe, 'Ginger [the rabbit] might eat them.'

We eventually decided on a site near the nature area and Phoebe used her trowel to make the small holes to put the plants in. After planting a few, Phoebe spotted a caterpillar. She picked it up and started to examine its properties. Theo came over to investigate, with Charlie following close behind.

'Can I have a look?' asked Theo. He looked closely at the caterpillar.

'I like him, it's wiggly, ahh he's going to bite me.'

'He won't bite, he hasn't got any teeth' said Phoebe, examining closer still.

Theo sat next to Phoebe who was still focused on the caterpillar.

'Shall we make him a house? He needs somewhere to sleep', Phoebe suggested.

'We need one of those big leaves' she said, as she picked a dock leaf and laid the caterpillar on it.

'He needs some grass now' she said

Theo and Phoebe worked together as they pulled up some grass and laid it carefully around him on the leaf. Phoebe and Theo were smiling with satisfaction at their caterpillar bed and really laughed as the caterpillar wriggled on it. Theo and Phoebe sat together watching the caterpillar move on the leaf and showing other interested children and adults what they had found. They soon had numerous visitors to see the caterpillar.

**Figure 5.6**  Phoebe, Theo and the caterpillar

**Figure 5.7**  Helping Karl

**Figure 5.8**  Playing with intelligent materials

**Table 5.5** Mapping and observation of Phoebe on the EYFS

| PERSONAL, SOCIAL AND EMOTIONAL DEVELOPMENT | COMMUNICATION, LANGUAGE AND LITERACY | PROBLEM SOLVING, REASONING AND NUMERACY | KNOWLEDGE AND UNDERSTANDING OF THE WORLD | PHYSICAL DEVELOPMENT, MOVEMENT AND SPACE | CREATIVE DEVELOPMENT RESPONDING TO EXPERIENCES AND EXPRESSING AND COMMUNICATING IDEAS |
|---|---|---|---|---|---|
| • **Dispositions and attitudes**<br>• **Self-confidence and self-esteem**<br>• **Making relationships**<br>• Behaviour and self-control<br>• Self-care<br>• Sense of community | • **Language for communication**<br>• **Language for thinking**<br>• Linking sounds and letters<br>• Reading<br>• Writing<br>• Handwriting | • Numbers as labels and for counting<br>• **Calculating**<br>• **shape, space and measures** | • **Exploration and investigation**<br>• **Designing and making**<br>• ICT<br>• Time<br>• Place<br>• **Communities** | • Health and bodily awareness<br>• **Using equipment and materials** | • **Exploring** media **and materials**<br>• Creating music and dance<br>• **Developing imagination and imaginative play** |

**Bold** indicates areas of progress made by Phoebe

## What next?

We have started to develop Forest School provision on our site. We have completed the first stage which gives us another workshop adjacent to woodland, a fire pit area, two tepees, a wild flower area with seating and a changing area for boots and wet suits. All children at the Foundation stage now have access to the 'Place of Possibilities' and a Forest School session each week. We never stand still at Leighswood and I am honoured to work with such fantastic practitioners and inspirational management.

## Resources

The resources required for this project are set out in Table 5.6.

**Table 5.6**   Project resources

| PEOPLE | FINANCES |
|---|---|
| Head teacher<br>Teacher in nursery<br>Teacher in children's centre<br>Children's centre manager<br>All Foundation Stage practitioners<br>Artists<br>Parents<br>Children | The total cost was £20,000 made up from Grants from the Big Lottery Fund for capital costs and Creative Partnerships for artists fees<br>Contribution from school budget to make up the difference |
| STAFF TIME | CHANGES TO SCHOOL ROUTINE |
| Release time for teacher to plan before and during the project<br>Evaluation and reflection time during the project<br>Planning time, for all involved<br>Assessment was part of normal nursery practice | Meetings before and after school to fit in with artist's workload<br>Arrangements made on weekly basis according to need |
| OTHER RESOURCES | SITES VISITED |
| Tools, machinery and resources sourced by artists<br>Adaptability of staff and children during construction of space<br>Enthusiasm and energy … and plenty of it | http://www.bloomsbury.bham.sch.uk/<br>http://www.bmag.org.uk/<br>http://www.ldelissa.bham.sch.uk/<br>http://www.pennhall.co.uk/<br>http://www.kingswood.herts.sch.uk |

## Questions for further discussion

1.  Looking at your site and your curriculum, what opportunities do you have to develop outdoor learning and in particular children's creativity?
2.  The school used close observation of children to find out what engaged them in the outdoor space. How would you audit and assess this in your setting?

3. Leighswood followed a carefully phased design process involving a range of people. How might you make use of their experience in your own setting?

4. Children were asked to shape the project before and during the construction of the new space. What is your settings' attitude to children's involvement? How might you use children as a resource?

5. What elements of Leighswood's space give opportunities for each new group of children that encounter it to make it their own? What else could they do to ensure that it has the 'capacity for re-invention' and how might you use that in your environment?

6. What do you think matters most to Leighswood's success: the space itself and materials provided, the way in which learning is organised or the approach of the staff?

7. The EYFS was used as the key framework for objectively assessing impact on children's learning. What other measures could you use in making judgements about the value of both the project and long term impact?

8. How could you do something like this with older or other age groups?

# 6

# Dangerous conversations

## Rebekah Hooper, Lakers School

## Editor's introduction

This case study describes a collective effort to develop creative classrooms across a whole secondary school and how young people were an integral part of the change process and in creating a new ethos in school. It looks at change at the individual and personal level and highlights the critical factors of building relationships, emotional and social intelligence amongst staff and students in creating the environment for sustainability. The elements of their challenge can be characterised as:

- the need to challenge pupil passivity;
- the need to revitalise staff morale and motivation;
- the aspiration to develop a curriculum that excites and engages;
- the need to transform teacher and pupil relationships.

Rebekah focuses in particular on how the school engaged teachers and how they found the energy and commitment to be motivated to make the changes they knew were required.

## Who's who?

- *Rebekah Hooper* lead teacher
- *Alison Elliott* head teacher
- *Staff team of 12* including teachers of English, Maths, Science, Art, Music, Drama, Geography, the librarian, two teaching assistants, technology technician and display technician
- *25 Year 8 students* BCreative research team
- *Diana Bogie* creative agent
- *Liz Morris and Heather Jenkins* The School of Emotional Literacy

## Timeline

- *September 2004* Initial weekly discussion and breakfast planning meetings involving staff team.
- *October 2004* Interviews and setting up of student team.
- *October 2004–April 2005* Regular discussion and planning meetings in various combinations of teams and individuals as felt necessary. Team building day for staff and students. Monthly training sessions for staff on emotional intelligence. training days for students and staff. Workshops and meetings for parents of student team with all staff and partners.
- *April–July 2005* Intensive planning for delivery of 7UP in September term and for Edinburgh conference with staff and students.
- *September 2005–July 2006* Delivery of 7UP – weekly team meetings at lunchtimes with whole day every term for review and planning. During this time, individual coaching and mentoring sessions were running. Edinburgh conference in October.

## The school context and key issues

- *Name* Lakers School, Business and Enterprise College
- *Location* Coleford, Gloucestershire
- *Age range* 11–16
- *No on roll* 765
- *Website* www.lakers.gloucs.sch.uk

Lakers School serves a catchment around the town of Coleford in the Forest of Dean. In choosing Business and Enterprise with the Rural Dimension as its specialism, the school has placed itself as a hub within the community to act as an agent for change in the regeneration of the local area. Almost all our students are white British with a few from other cultural backgrounds. A quarter of our students are SEN including some with statements and many of our families have a narrow experience beyond the local area and so have a limited engagement with different communities.

I have been a teacher at Lakers School for 14 years. When I first took up a post as head of Music, Lakers was a school with some of the best contextual value added results in the county, and a reputation for providing high quality education for the local community. I was proud and excited to be working there.

Then for a period of five years our school went into serious decline resulting in an inspection that rated the school as having serious issues and requiring rapid improvement. In a relatively short space of time we had become the 'sink school' with widespread withdrawal of support from our local community and under regular external scrutiny.

With the appointment of a new head teacher we improved to be judged by Inspectors as a 'good' school in 18 months. To achieve this meant being ruled by systems, driven by targets and data and working in a culture which demanded consistency with every lesson in every subject delivered in the same format. Learning objectives and outcomes became our mantra. Learning in our school had become dull and formulaic.

> We never had the time to take risks in the classroom – I felt guilty if I went off at a tangent or didn't follow my lesson plan.
>
> Ros Howden, English teacher

Staff morale was low, retention poor and those of us left wondered what had gone wrong. We blamed it on leadership, students and government initiatives; in fact we blamed it on anyone and anything. All that was left was a culture of blame and a hard core of staff who had once been celebrated as 'the best' feeling let down and many disillusioned with the profession and some ready to leave. I had stepped down from my middle leadership role as head of Expressive Arts and was looking for a career change.

Students were becoming increasingly disengaged; passive recipients in the classroom with fixed expectations around the roles of the teacher and student – masters at blame and many lacking the skills they needed to succeed without teachers leading. Along with colleagues, I often pondered that it might be easier to take the 30 GCSEs myself rather than coax, drive and cajole, weary mistrustful and bored students to achieve their 'potential'.

Teachers dreamt of classes full of motivated, independent and creative learners who could think and do for themselves. Students wanted interesting lessons and good relationships with their teachers. We were stuck. What else could we do and where else was there for us to go?

Does this pattern of rapid improvement, reaching a plateau and getting stuck seem familiar to you? How easy it is to be as honest as the writer is here about the causes?

## The development process

At about the same time two key initiatives arrived in school; Guy Claxton's work on 'Building Learning Power' and Creative Partnerships. I had decided to get involved with the Guy Claxton work as it encouraged me to think about what good teaching and learning looked like. I was interested in his emphasis on developing good learning habits in students, such as resilience, resourcefulness, independence and how good learning happens. It made me appraise how I behaved as a teacher and the relationship I had with the pupils; did I need to feel I was always in control and setting the agenda? I decided to negotiate with my class and seek their feedback about my lessons and learning in my classroom. I was frankly terrified to begin with and at the same time liberated by the whole process. I felt that at last there was some integrity in my classroom with learning becoming a shared process even with the potential minefields and tricky negotiations ahead of me. I took away a clear insight – I can and should learn from my pupils.

My first response to Creative Partnerships (CP) was 'so what's new?' Initiative fatigue and cynicism were quick to kick in and this is not entirely to my credit. However the strength of CP was that it was a far remove from the 'top down' initiatives we had become used to and it presented us with a refreshing opportunity to try something new, take some risks with the time, money and support to do it. I was appointed coordinator for our programme and through conversations with colleagues I was convinced that if we could look in depth at issues around learning rather than run individual projects, it might help us to understand the reasons for the lack of sustained whole school improvement.

I met with my head teacher and outlined my ambition for our work which really was about developing in our pupils the positive attitudes and good habits of learning. I also wanted this change to be led by ordinary teachers, not have it imposed upon us, so we put together a cross curricular team of teachers and other adults who met on a weekly basis for at least an hour over seven months. Originally made up of subject leaders, the team embraced those who chose to take part and included support staff, a key check on 'how things really are'. Whilst their inclusion was questioned by some staff at the outset, it became clear that support staff were going to be an invaluable resource.

> I am excited about having the opportunity to work more closely with the students in my current position. I don't often get the chance (or time) to work closely with them. This has give me the opportunity to work as part of a team and I have found it very stimulating, it's something I don't get to experience in a lone position in the school.
>
> Kate Williams, Librarian

The early meetings provided an important way of engaging adults in school who had felt disengaged and whose morale had reached a low point. There were concerns that such meetings would spiral into negativity due to the initial lack of familiarity around what we were going to do and how we were going to do. It was a risk, but a necessary one as there was a need for staff to re-engage with the whole school agenda and to feel included in that change.

Our creative agent, Diana Bogie was an integral part of the team. She became a catalyst for much of my thinking and helped to move things along practically too. She was essential in that she provided me with a link to the world beyond Lakers; she gave me reading, stimuli and shared experiences in other schools and settings. She was an independent agent who could negotiate between me and school if any difficult situations arose and broker outside partners. She made the whole process run smoothly and gave me the confidence to lead the work.

In attempting a significant change, the role of the external advisor/critical friend is held here to be vital, especially with the staff group. Is this always needed or can you find these resources within the school? Is it the person or the role?

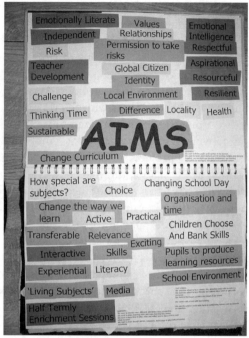

**Figure 6.1**   Rebekah's learning journal

We agreed on a core question to drive our work. What would our Dream School be like; the ideal student, the ideal teacher, the ideal learning environment? We held project development days for the team to be off timetable and off site; initially facilitated by Diane but less so as we became clearer about what we wanted to do.

In a hands-on, practical and fun way we were became learners again, struggling with the complexities of teaching and learning. For instance we used digital technology to create short films and animations and we were challenged to think creatively, try out new things and were taken out of our comfort zones on team-building days. The process was invigorating and reminded us what it was about teaching and learning that we loved, re-vitalising a team of committed professionals.

Through this time together we identified key attributes for the ideal learner: aspirational, confident, flexible, independent, motivated, articulate, resilient and creative. Our ambition was to support young people to develop a set of generic learning skills that would underpin subject learning and is now incorporated in the concept of personal learning and thinking skills (PLTs) We wanted learners to understand their strengths and weaknesses and use a 'learner profile' which could be built on from Year 7 and equip them with skills for life.

It became evident through the process how frustrated the team were by a formulaic approach to teaching which left little room for real interaction with students. Our time together gave them scope to express their ambitions and what motivated them.

I want to have time for discussion and questioning without feeling pressured to provide evidence for SLT to monitor. I want to try to provoke a true love of learning and discovery in the pupils that I teach. I want a classroom atmosphere where ideas are shared, valued and made reality.

Natasha Phillips, Maths teacher

Teaching for creativity is presented here as being about fun, generic learning skills and a classroom environment in which discoveries can be made, ideas explored and valued. Do you agree? Is there anything else involved? Is fun the same thing as engagement?

It became apparent that any work around learning must involve students, so we recruited a team of students who would work with us as co-researchers. This group of 20 students included highly motivated, high achieving students and those disengaged with low self-esteem, low aspirations and several students at risk of exclusion. Students Charlotte Morgan and Lorna Russell explain:

We didn't know much about what to expect but soon realised we could finally make a difference to school life. We realised that students weren't actively engaged in their learning and didn't have a say in the running of the school, as all decisions were made by senior staff and governors. We set up a group called 'Bcreative' and started to ask questions abut learning in our school.

- What were the bad things about our lessons and the teachers?
- What would we like to change?
- What would our Dream School look like?

After a considerable amount of thought and research we came up with a long list of what we wanted to change in our school but we didn't think anyone would listen to us. When we were asked about what we wanted to happen at the school, some ideas were surprising and radical – from adding escalators to burning down the building! Once we thought in depth about the questions we realised our ideas were not that different from those of the staff. We agreed on things such as:

- cross-curricular learning; longer blocks of time; better relationships with teachers;
- more outdoor and interactive learning; more hands on learning; more experts from outside school working with us – make learning real; more choice and control over our learning'.

How much space and freedom is it possible to give young people as researchers on their own school? What happens when findings are presented that are not welcome or views are expressed in ways that are challenging?

## Next steps

With a clear idea of what we wanted to achieve, our CP office recommended Liz Morris and Heather Jenkins from the School of Emotional Literacy to work with us on creating a learning environment that cared for staff and students' emotional well-being. There were some important and immediate developments as a result of their involvement.

Liz and Heather acted as coaches and mentors for the staff including some extra support for me and the head teacher instigated a process of action research and provided training around concepts of Emotional Intelligence (EI) which were concerned with an awareness of self and one's impact on others. They also worked with parents and students around EI concepts and challenged our perceptions of traditional teacher-student models. I was also given a day and a half a week off timetable to lead and develop the work which was beginning to build momentum. We articulated our work through a vision statement we titled 'Radical change in a learning organisation' as follows:

> Using an ongoing process of consultation, reflection, action/experimentation, review, consultation reflection etc. (a process that follows the action research and action learning methodology) we will engage in an extended process of dialogue and discussion between all parties in the community. Through this process we aim to understand the needs, hopes, fears and wishes of all the stakeholders in the school community regarding their learning experience at Lakers. By facilitating this genuine and rigorous consultation and reflection and through the action research process of implementation, which ensures organic and natural extension, we can begin to build secure powerful relationships and gain more and more clarity and confidence in our actions. We will therefore enable our organisation to effect change from within that is both sustainable and transformational at many levels.

How useful do you see the process of crafting a vision statement in your context? Does this one give you a sense of the purpose and drive of the project?

The involvement of our head teacher, Alison Elliott, was critical to the in depth development work being realised in curriculum change. However she reveals the nature of her dilemma and how additional 'thinking' support gave her the resolve to support us to lead change:

> The context of lack of low aspirations, low self-esteem, low literacy rates and poor attitudes to learning present both an opportunity for radically different approaches and a real threat. Achievement and attainment could be argued to be too fragile for us to take a risk. The attitude we adopted was to face the fact that the traditional curriculum route has not been engaging sufficient learners and has not unlocked additional motivation from colleagues. The timely questions from Liz prompt a depth of analysis and reflection that I

would not access without her support. The relationship that has developed has been critical for me in boosting my confidence and giving me permission to innovate. In turn I have been enabled to pass on this heightened confidence to colleagues, to students and so to our learning community in its broadest sense.

How important is gaining 'permission' to innovate? What else is needed?

## The 7UP programme

Our first tangible step to developing creative classrooms was with Year 7, which established the principles of all our subsequent developments. Pupils Charlotte Morgan and Lorna Russell of the BCreative research team describe it:

We developed a programme of study for new students arriving at the school for the duration of their first year. This comprised of one morning a week (four hours) devoted to projects based upon the theme of identity explored through music, art, creative writing and website design.

The group began as a diverse range of students from all backgrounds and abilities and staff from all areas of the school- teachers, technology assistants and display technicians. After a year we were asked to present our ideas at a national conference in Edinburgh, in which we showed how adding creativity to learning helped enthuse students and create a more interesting learning environment.

From our point of view, the young people were really the driving force in the group. We spent time documenting and researching how the project was impacting the school and how we could further improve initiatives we had began to roll out across year groups. It was important to get the viewpoints of the students who were affected by our project, so we could continually try to improve and add to our work.

Each session focused on activities around key questions of identity. Students chose what they wanted to do and how to present their projects. As many were used to being directed by adults or merely compliant in the classroom they needed considerable support in the initial stages of negotiating and understanding the potential of 'freedom', choice and flexibility. This required considerable input from staff as coaches and facilitators and required us to rapidly develop new skills in these roles. This way of working represented a paradigm shift for teachers and students.

How would you find the right balance of offering freedom and providing constraints to pupils in a task designed to develop creative learning? What more is needed to build children's confidence to form their own opinions and realise their ideas? How important are the development of specific skills to this?

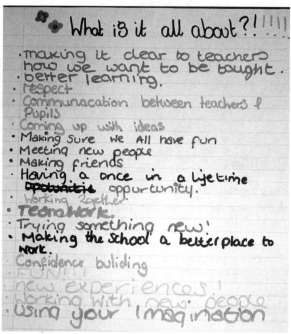

**Figure 6.2**  Explaining 7UP

**Figure 6.3**  The rules for 7UP

## Involving creative practitioners

We involved the expertise of a wide range of creative practitioners to support the delivery of 7UP and so we could offer film-making, radio production, dance, song writing, web design, teambuilding, outdoor learning, photography and animation. Alongside this, there was an intensive coaching and professional development programme for all staff around the principles and practice of Social, Emotional

**Figure 6.4** Identity imagery

Aspects of Learning (SEAL)[1] which we were now convinced was central to developing a shared ethos.

## More time

In a weekly four hour block there was time to learn alongside one another and ask questions together. Confrontation, dispute and challenge were managed more effectively, resulting in more secure working relationships between adults and students. Pacing learning over four hour sessions is complex. There are ebbs and flows of energy and clear 'up' and 'down' times. The beauty of this time is that there are opportunities to negotiate ways through 'blocks' to learning so enabling students to become reflective learners who can begin to take more responsibility. Students commented on the importance of this sustained period of time to enable them to experiment, immerse themselves in an activity and return to it:

It's having the time to make a mistake and then put it right; the time to talk to people about things that aren't going so well.

I can really get into something and not worry about the bell going.

I can break up the time how I want to – so if I need a bit of a break after an hour I can but if I want to just keep going that's OK too.

In this space students and teachers interacted differently, or more importantly 'normally', in a real life context. We engaged in conversations around learning and focused on the process of learning and how students felt about themselves as individuals.

## Commitment to research and reflection

Everyone completed journals or 'learning logs' as a method of reflection and a record of the project and we set aside time at the end of every session for the students. The BCreative Research Team documented every session and reported back to us. We met every week to reflect on what we had done well, what we could do better next time and we always acted on our observations.

## Building relationships and developing emotional intelligence

We spent time building and nurturing relationships, negotiating circle time boundaries, creating routines and rituals. We worked hard to create an environment in which students felt safe enough to take risks in their learning and on a personal level. Students warmed to teachers who were prepared to take risks alongside them, to share their own experiences and to simply be themselves. This is a more demanding and challenging way of being in the classroom and requires a high degree of social and emotional awareness, and inter/intrapersonal skills. Over time the 'code of conduct' that we established was one based on a clear set of rigorous expectations and a code of meaningful human values.

## What happened?

## Enhanced learner confidence and positive attitudes to learning

Many Year 7 students demonstrated significantly higher levels of confidence and we had never enjoyed such high levels of appropriate assertiveness from our students. The English staff commented that children who previously wouldn't speak were more articulate and engaged in speaking and listening activities. Outside visitors such as our volunteer careers advisors observed the increased willingness of pupils to contribute ideas and work independently. This kind of feedback gave us confidence that we were making progress.

Most students (and I must recognise here that a small percentage found the experience very challenging) demonstrated a genuine engagement in their learning, sharing a sense of excitement and an eagerness to communicate both the process and quality. Most notable was the increase in student resilience and pride in the way that they had sustained their own learning. The opportunity for collaboration at all levels proved to be very profound in terms of moving student-to-student relationships forward. The desire to 'buy into' the success that other groups or individuals were having became one of the key motivating factors. There were also significant developments in all students' willingness and capacity to 'dig deeper', to analyse their own learning processes and to explore ideas in a more complex and thoughtful way.

## Skills development

Students talked far more readily, with a greater amount of eye contact and with a broader vocabulary. This was particularly evident in the levels of active listening and participation in circle time with pupils far more willing to explore ideas rather than to give a limited and nervous response. Interaction between students in the 7UP session meant that they more readily backed each other up when responding and their emphasis was on co-operation rather than competition. Students developed skills in art forms such as: photography, film, song writing, drama, dance, sculpture, animation, comic strips, poetry and storytelling. We created our very own 7UP outdoor classroom and our creative partners helped us to develop the potential of using the locality and environment as a natural extension of the classroom.

## The opportunity for adults to become reflective learners

The process of change was rigorous and challenging and it demanded all stakeholders to shape the work and take responsibility. This was socially complex and required the development of skills in social and emotional competencies and a high degree of self-awareness. There is clear evidence that those teachers who participated have taken these new skills back to their 'everyday' classroom as students have openly commented on the change in attitude of these teachers and we have data that shows improved results. My results certainly improved because I took an entirely different approach with a potentially difficult and challenging GCSE group. Support staff that worked with students in a more personally challenging way proved to be effective leaders in the classroom and now lead initiatives in our school.

**Figure 6.5**   A finished product

## Conclusion

I found myself in a unique position in my school. I was not a member of the senior leadership team and had chosen to step down from a middle leadership role but through my new role had an insight into leadership that challenged my own perceptions of who could influence, shape and lead an organisation. Improving my school was as much about the students leading alongside me as it was the domain of the senior leaders.

I learnt that any voice, be it student, teacher or adult in the organisation must be authentic, and any change, if it is to be sustainable and transformational must be organic, rooted in that community and responding to the needs of all learners.

This approach demands honesty, integrity and open lines of communication – even when the messages are sometimes 'difficult to hear'. In terms of hard data we are now five years in and our results have improved year on year. Although this is due to a combination of factors there is evidence to suggest that we have moved on from a series of creative initiatives across the school to it becoming an approach which has impacted on whole school improvement. Our 2009 results were the highest in the history of our school with the least likely cohort. To us, it was a minor miracle.

Much of what we were doing questioned traditional secondary educational norms and models and the process of change was exhilarating, gruelling and often isolating. It demanded high degrees of persistence, self-belief and pure dogged determination. The process changed me and the kind of teacher that I am now.

## Resources

The resources required for this project are set out in Table 6.1.

**Table 6.1**  Project resources

| PEOPLE | RESOURCES/FINANCES |
| --- | --- |
| All partners and whole team | Over the first two years the funding amounted to £35,000 from Creative Partnerships and school contributions. Broken down, the major part went to partners and then staff time – the next biggest expense. The journals for students were the only major capital expense and some materials for art. |
| TIME | CHANGES TO SCHOOL ROUTINES |
| Release time for staff team<br>One day per term for planning<br>Twilight and half-hour sessions for staff training and mentoring sessions<br>Staff gave up considerable time of their own for early morning and lunchtime meetings and of course individual planning | Change of timetable to include a 4 hour block in Year 7 and cross-curricular team of staff<br>Ensuring continuity when large staff teams were off normal timetable; implications for continuity and learning. This needs to be handled carefully and with consideration |

## Questions for further discussion

1. To what extent are the challenges Rebekah diagnosed similar to yours? Where are the area of resonance and dissonance?

2. The opportunity to initiate change came through the enterprising use of 'initiatives' – what such opportunities exist in your school that might give permission to work in new ways and take purposeful risks?

3. The case study shows the potential for young people to be an integral part of a curriculum change. What is required to give a dynamic voice to young people and the power to influence? Is this always possible or desirable? How might you deal with things you don't want to hear?

4. Lakers began with teachers and students on a journey of discovery. In a world of SMART (Specific, Measurable, Achievable, Realistic, Time limited) objectives how would you argue for time and resources for a project which begins with no idea of where it might go or what might result?

5. External creative practitioners and advisors were an important source of ideas and support to Lakers. How might you access and make use of such external support?

# Appendix

## Engaging learners

*Purpose*   To consider the features of the learning environment that engages learners

*Time required*   1–2 hours

*Participants*   Whole staff

*Outline of activity*   To promote analysis and discussion about the different features of a learning environment that encourages creative learning and so engages learners

*Resources*   Copies of the six case studies plus the introduction; post-it notes in three colours. A long roll of lining paper divided into three sections with headings of physical environment, social and power relationships, emotional environment

*Instructions*
*30 minutes:* Divide the group into at least seven smaller groups and ask each group to read a different case study or the introduction. As they read through the case studies ask the groups to identify the different features of the learning environment under the headings physical environment, social and power relationships, emotional environment, using a different colour post-it note for each heading.

*5 minutes:* Once the groups have completed the reading, roll out the lining paper in the centre of the room and ask the groups to place their post-it notes under the appropriate categories

*15 minutes:* Ask the groups to arrange the post-it notes into common themes and patterns and then discuss the relationships that have emerged. What do they notice?

*10 minutes:* Conclude with a discussion of how these might relate or compare to current practice in school

*Further development*

Extend the time for analysis and discussion. Audit the features of the school environment in the light of this analysis – what emerges as the most promising area for development? Agree three actions that can be taken forward.

# The contribution of creative practitioners

*Purpose*   To identify the contribution of creative practitioners to new creative pedagogical practice

*Time required*   1–2 hours

*Participants*   Whole staff or smaller staff teams

*Outline of activity*   To identify the role, skills and dispositions that creative practitioners bring to the development of creative learning and discuss what is required for staff to work effectively with them

*Resources*

Copies of the six case studies (but in particular Allens Croft, Deansfield and Brannel for smaller groups); post-it notes; large sheets of plain paper.

*Instructions*

Divide the group into six smaller groups (or three for smaller group) working at least in pairs

*30 minutes.* Ask groups to read a different case study and then discuss it with their partner, noting down on the paper or on post-it notes the following as they read through:

■   What did the creative practitioners bring that was different to teachers?
■   How did staff work most effectively with the partners?
■   What was required to make the partnership work?

*10 minutes.* Ask for contributions from the groups under each heading to build a group analysis. Summarise the key aspects.

*20 minutes.* Divide the whole group into different groups of five or so. Using the analysis, set each group the task of creating a brief that will attract a creative practitioner to work in their area of the school, setting out working processes and expectations. Share out and note the characteristics of one most likely to excite and engage a creative practitioner.

*Further development*

Identify what the teacher/teaching assistant brings, what the child brings and what the creative practitioner brings to a partnership. Look in the case studies to see how these have been honoured in successful projects.

Select one of the sample projects generated by the group, work it up more fully, identify resources and actually make it happen. Report back to the whole group on what is learned.

## The role and requirement of senior leaders

*Purpose*   To consider the role and requirements of senior leaders in supporting staff to develop creative learning

*Time required*   2 hours

*Participants*   Senior leaders

*Outline of activity*   To engage senior leaders and others who manage classroom practitioners to consider how to promote risk taking and a culture of disciplined innovation.

*Resources*   Copies of the six case studies plus the introduction; school vision statement and curriculum policy; post-it notes in three colours; large sheets of plain paper; a white board marked out in three columns labelled motivation, voice and leadership action for course leader to display post-it notes.

*Instructions*

*20 minutes*: Review the curriculum or pedagogic innovations that the school has introduced in the last three years. Consider the scale of these innovations, how risky these felt when they were introduced and how much of a risk they feel now. Consider what determined whether these innovations succeeded or failed.

*20 minutes:* Consider how easy was it to introduce each innovation and what that might say about the schools attitude to risk and change. Rate your school's attitude to risk on a scale of 1–10 (1 being extremely risk averse, 10 extremely risk tolerant) and justify your rating.

*30 minutes*: Share the case studies out amongst the team. Read each through noting how the school introduced new practice and their approach to risk. In particular note how and why the senior management supported the project. Discuss these and see what commonalities emerged.

*10 minutes*: Apply this analysis to your school's rationale for developing creative learning. Discuss and note how it connects with the school's vision and core purposes.

*20 minutes*: Consider priority areas in the school for a 'disciplined creative learning innovation' and agree what this term might mean. Discuss what success and failure might mean, and in particular the value of failure for learning. Look at what the case studies show about senior management behaviours that are most likely to support innovation.

*20–30 minutes.* Create an advert to invite teachers/staff to apply in pairs for a creative learning project with a 'permission to innovate', identifying the criteria, resources and support you will provide and the expectations of the teachers in return.

*Further development*

Circulate the advert the group is most excited by and run a process for teachers to apply, interview them and award a 'permission to innovate' with resources and assign a senior management 'angel' to support them. See what happens and share it.

## The introduction of creative learning

*Purpose*   To consider the key knowledge, skills and behaviours that teachers need to introduce creative learning

*Time required*   2½ hours

*Participants*   Whole staff or smaller staff teams

*Outline of activity*   To build a profile that teachers understand of the knowledge, skills and behaviours needed to lead creative learning

*Resources*   Flip chart paper and pens, blu-tack, post-it notes and sheets of blank paper, copies of six case studies

*Instructions*

*20 minutes.* As a whole group make a list of 'what makes a good teacher' under the three headings of skills, knowledge and behaviours, using one piece of flip chart for each heading. Attach each piece to the wall. (This can also be done in pairs or small groups depending on group size)

*40 minutes.* Divide the group into at least seven groups and share out the case studies plus the introduction. Using the same headings as above use the evidence of the case studies to make a list of 'what enables a teacher to teach for pupil creativity?' Implicit in this discussion is each group discussing and defining what pupil creativity means to them.

*20 minutes.* Ask each group to share their deliberations and record responses to each heading on a separate piece of flip chart paper. Stick them by the corresponding paper from the first exercise to allow easy comparison. Explore the commonalities and differences between the two lists of 'a good teacher' and a 'teacher that teaches for pupil creativity'.

*20 minutes.* Lead a discussion using findings from the case studies on the following:

- What was required for the teachers to develop new skills and confidence?
- Where did they start? What was crucial to them getting going? Where did they get ideas?

*30–40 minutes*: In small groups prepare a presentation to convince senior management to support a pilot creative learning project – identifying professional development needs, potential partnerships, resources required and what success might look like.

*10 minutes*: Share the presentations

*10 minutes*: Reflect on the session and agree two actions that can be implemented

*Further development*

Using the lists defined by staff and through additional reading of the literature on teaching for creativity devise a guide for teachers to develop their own creative pedagogy that can be used to inform professional development, lesson planning and peer observation.

Use this guide as an audit and planning tool for staff development.

## Methodology and reflection

My intention in commissioning the chapters for this book was to offer the reader multiple perspectives and points of connection to the core question about how to develop a creative classroom and the different dimensions that need to be considered. It seemed important to me to represent the findings of teachers and practitioners across the phases of education to challenge the notion that playfulness and creativity is what happens before the serious business of academic work takes over.

I found the authors through a mixture of luck and judgement. All of them are involved in the Creative Partnerships programme. Some I knew personally from my time working for Creative Partnerships and others were recommended by colleagues in different parts of the country. From a long list of potential contributors the six authors were confirmed once they had submitted a 200 word proposal. We then went through a process of writing, re-drafting and dialogue to uncover the core ideas we thought would engage the reader and then refined the focus, narrative flow and depth of reflection to meet the brief from the series editors to 'say a lot about a little'. While most of the featured schools are in areas of disadvantage the authors stayed away from 'deficit' language – i.e. focussing on what children and communities can't do - and this has been used only as a contextual factor in shaping the choices that were made.

A key concern for me was to encourage a distinctive and personal voice in each case study and to make the writers feel confident that what they had to say was of interest to other colleagues. In structuring each case study to agree to a common format I hope the personality of the writer has been preserved.

In producing this book it has been a privilege to have had the chance to reflect in depth with such an informed and thoughtful team and this includes the authors and editors of the accompanying volumes on creative learning and leadership, young people's voice and special educational needs. It may be that as writers we will have learned the most from the discipline of writing and being challenged to articulate how and what we know. So I suggest you be encouraged by this and take every opportunity to write, present and share your insights into your practice. I noticed that apart from the Brannel teachers (Chapter 2) who had undertaken research training, the artists and creative practitioners found it more natural than the teachers involved to analyse and write about their work. Reflective practice tends to form an integral part of their training and working practices and to secure work they have to be able to articulate what and how they work to potential clients. This is a tangible and often overlooked quality that they bring to partnerships with staff and children.

There are two further thoughts that come to mind from the process of editing this volume. The first is the necessity of diversity to the creative process. New practices and understandings are only made possible by being open and alert to the possibilities offered by the unusual and the counter-intuitive. Seeking out these people and ideas requires an active connection and curiosity about the world and the need to take risks to engage with them. My second reflection is the need to talk about and so be precise about what is meant by creative learning and to keep articulating the value it brings to school life and to young people's achievements. This way there is a chance that children and young people's right to a creative and cultural education will become part of the fabric of education.

# Notes

## Introduction

1  See OfSTED themed reports *Learning, Creative Approaches that Raise Standards* (2010) and *Creative Partnerships: Initiative and Impact* (2006) http://www.ofsted.gov.uk/

2  For a more detailed exploration of this debate a good place to start is with the writings of Anna Craft. See *Creativity in Schools, Tensions and Dilemmas* in the References list.

3  See http://www.learnnc.org/lp/pages/939 for a short introduction.

## 2  Active approaches to teaching

1  The LPN is a national programme run by the RSC began in 2006 that aims to transform the teaching and learning of Shakespeare around the principles of 'active approaches' inspired by the rehearsal room practice of the company. It involves clusters of schools working together over a three year partnership with the RSC to engage in a programme of CPD, create and run a Shakespeare festival and further performance opportunities for young people. A distinctive feature is that two teachers from the 'hub' school of each cluster pursue an action research project to qualify for a postgraduate certificate with the University of Warwick.

2  *Times Educational Supplement Magazine*, article undated

3  Michael Boyd, Artistic Director of the RSC defines ensemble as the 'collective enquiry' of a company working together over an extended period of time, up to three years at the RSC, to make deep connections to the plays and to each other and by establishing mutual trust take creative risks that enable artistic achievements.

4  Source: pupil interview for action research project.

5  This is a dialogic strategy that develops a precise understanding of the thoughts and words of a character. It involves pupils responding to provoking questions from the teacher using the original text and is particularly effective in engaging with the complexity of a soliloquy.

6  Source: pupil interview for action research project.

## 3 Ensuring equality with a focus on boys' learning

1  http://nationalstrategies.standards.dcsf.gov.uk/node/153355

## 4 The neighbourhood classroom

1  http://curriculum.qcda.gov.uk/key-stages-3-and-4/skills/personal-learning-and-thinking-skills/index.aspx
2  The school was placed in an OfSTED category called special measures which judged the school as inadequate and therefore had to rapidly improve or potentially face closure.

## 5 The place of possibilities

1  Children's Centres are an England wide network of centres designed to 'provide multi-agency services that are flexible and meet the needs of young children and their families. The core offer includes integrated early learning, care, family support, health services, outreach services to children and families not attending the Centre and access to training and employment advice.' http://www.childrens-centres.org/
2  For further information on Reggio Emilia see the Reggio Children site http://zerosei.comune.re.it/ and http://www.sightlines-initiative.com the UK reference point for Reggio Children which seeks to promote and disseminate the development of their approach to early years pedagogy.
3  See resources section at the end of this case study for references.

## 6 Dangerous conversations

1  SEAL is 'a framework for explicitly promoting social, emotional and behavioural skills in pupils, with built-in progression for each year group within a school'. These skills are identified as self-awareness, managing feelings, motivation, empathy, social skills. See http://nationalstrategies.standards.dcsf.gov.uk/node/65860?uc=force_uj

# References

## Introduction

Banaji, S., Burn, A. and Buckingham, D. (2006) *The Rhetorics of Creativity: A Review of the Literature*. London: Creative Partnerships, Arts Council England.

Bentley, T. (1999) *The Creative Age: Knowledge and Skills for a New Economy*. London: Demos

Birkett, D. (5 June 2002) 'The Children's Manifesto', Education Guardian, The Guardian.

Boekarts, M. (2010) The Role of Motivation and Emotion in Classroom Learning, in Dumont, H., Istance, D., Benavides F. (eds) *The Nature of Learning, Using Research to Inspire Practice*. Paris: OECD, pp. 91–111.

Burke, C. and Grosvenor, I. (2003) *The School I'd Like, Children and Young People's Reflections on an Education for the 21st Century*. Abingdon: RoutledgeFalmer.

Craft, A. (2005) *Creativity in Schools, Tensions and Dilemmas*. Abingdon: Routledge.

Csíkszentmihályi, M. (1997) *Finding Flow: The Psychological Engagement with Everyday Life*. New York: Basic Books.

Department for Education and Skills (DfES) (2004) *Every Child Matters, Change for Children*. Nottingham: DfES.

Dickinson, R., Neelands J. and Shenton Primary School (2006) *Improve Your Primary School Through Drama*. London: David Fulton.

Fleming, M. (2008) *Arts in Education and Creativity: A Review of the Literature*. London: Creative Partnerships, Arts Council England.

Fullan, M. (2007) *The New Meaning of Educational Change*, fourth edition. Abingdon: Routledge.

González, N., Moll, L. and Amanti, C. (2005) *Funds of Knowledge: Theorizing Practices in Households, Communities, and Classrooms*. Mahwah: NJ: Lawrence Erlbaum Associates.

Kanter, R.M. (2004) *Confidence: How Winning and Losing Streaks Begin and End*. New York: Crown Business.

National Advisory Committee on Creative and Cultural Education (NACCCE) (1999) *All our Futures: Creativity, Culture and Education*. London: Department for Education and Employment.

Neelands, J. and Choe, B. (2010) The English Model of Creativity: Cultural Politics of An Idea, *International Journal of Cultural Policy*, 16 (3): 287–304.

Ruddock, J., Chaplain, R. and Wallace, G. (1996) *School Improvement: What can pupils tell us?* London: David Fulton.

Sefton Green, J. (2008) *Creative Learning*. London: Creative Partnerships, Arts Council England.

Thomson, P. (2007) *Whole School Change: A Review of The Literature*. London: Creative Partnerships, Arts Council England.

The Office for Standards in Education (OFSTED) (2010) *Learning: Creative Approaches that Raise Standards*. Manchester: OFSTED.

# Index

# Taylor & Francis

# eBooks
## FOR LIBRARIES

ORDER YOUR FREE 30 DAY INSTITUTIONAL TRIAL TODAY!

Over 23,000 eBook titles in the Humanities, Social Sciences, STM and Law from some of the world's leading imprints.

**Choose from a range of subject packages or create your own!**

Benefits for **you**

▶ Free MARC records

▶ COUNTER-compliant usage statistics

▶ Flexible purchase and pricing options

Benefits for your **user**

▶ Off-site, anytime access via Athens or referring URL

▶ Print or copy pages or chapters

▶ Full content search

▶ Bookmark, highlight and annotate text

▶ Access to thousands of pages of quality research at the click of a button

For more information, pricing enquiries or to order a free trial, contact your local online sales team.

UK and Rest of World: **online.sales@tandf.co.uk**

US, Canada and Latin America:
**e-reference@taylorandfrancis.com**

## www.ebooksubscriptions.com

ALPSP Award for BEST eBOOK PUBLISHER 2009 Finalist
sponsored by

Taylor & Francis eBooks
Taylor & Francis Group

A flexible and dynamic resource for teaching, learning and research.